THE PRACTICAL
KABBALAH
guidebook

THE PRACTICAL
KABBALAH
guidebook

C.J.M. HOPKING

GODSFIELD PRESS

First published in Great Britain in 2001
by Godsfield Press Ltd
A division of David and Charles Ltd
Brunel House, Forde Close, Newton Abbot,
Devon TQ12 4PU, UK

10 9 8 7 6 5 4 3 2 1

© 2001 Godsfield Press
Text © C. J. M. Hopking

Designed for Godsfield Press by
The Bridgewater Book Company

Picture research *Liz Moore*
Mac illustration *Mark Preston* and *Richard Lloyd*
Illustrations *Lesley Ann Hutchings*
Page layout *Janette Revill*

C. J. M. Hopking asserts the moral right
to be identified as the author of this work.

The publishers wish to thank the following for the use of pictures:
Bibliothèque de l'Arsenal, Paris: 103; Bridgeman Art Library:
7t, 10, 13, 85t, 92, 96t, 97t, 105t, 109b, 115b, 116, 122; Ashmolean
Museum: 11b; Baroda Museum: 107b; Cecil Higgins Art Gallery,
Bedford: 56; Christie's Images: 97b; Fitzwilliam Museum,
Cambridge: 101; Fogg Art Museum, Harvard University,
Cambridge, USA: 70; Osterreichische Galerie, Vienna, Austria:
2, 19; Royal Ontario Museum, Toronto: 107t; Pierpont Morgan
Library: 115t; Corbis UK Ltd: 7b, 11t, 12, 15, 17b, 18, 25b, 27t,
33t, 37, 71l, 98r, 111 both, 117; Bridgewater Picture Library: 36b;
Getty Stone: 23b, 39t, 105b; Sonia Halliday: 109t; Sarah Howerd:
95b; Image Bank: 23t, 38r, 44cb, 106br; Jewish National
University Library: 95t; NASA: 42, 48r, 50, 52b, 54bl; Zev
Radovan, Israel: 6, 8, 27b, 114; Science Photo Library: 21 both,
25t, 40, 46bl; Stadtbibliothek, Mainz: 84, 99b; Tibet Images: 100b;
Visconti-Sforza Tarot (c) 1975: 118 both.

*While every effort has been made to establish the copyright holder of all the
illustrations in this book, in some cases it has not been possible. We would
welcome any further information.*

Printed and bound in China
ISBN 1 84181 115 7

*Frontispiece: The Lord calls Moses to lead the children
of Israel out of Egypt. Moses and the Burning Bush
by Ernst Fuchs (b.1930) (detail).*

CONTENTS

Introduction

Certain questions—such as "Who am I?" and "Why am I here?"—are timeless. One aim of this book is to point the way to answers to such questions. Through the ages, the practice of Kabbalah has helped some men and women—people like you and me—find answers. All paths and teachings do this. Whether Kabbalah speaks more clearly to you than other paths is a matter of personal preference.

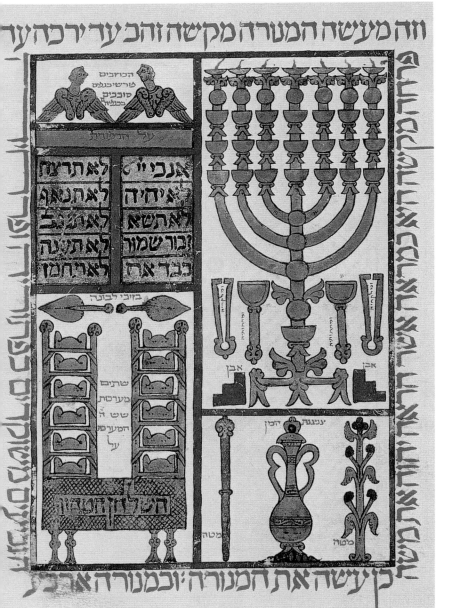

With its roots deep in the ancient Egyptian Mysteries, its branches intertwined through the magical and social history of Europe and North America, and its fruit being harvested to this day, the Kabbalah sits entirely within the spiritual traditions of the West. Kabbalah lies at the heart of the three main strands of Western spirituality. In this book, these three different versions of the same teaching are identified by three different spellings: Kabbalah, Cabala, and Qabalah.

Kabbalah Judaism

The Kabbalah is essentially a Jewish mystical or "esoteric" system. The 11th-century Spanish mystic Solomon Ibn Gabriol first named these teachings using the four Hebrew letters KBLH. Kabbalah can mean "from mouth to ear," or "the received wisdom," depending on the translation.

At some periods of history, study of the Kabbalah has been hidden away in the synagogue; at other periods it has been displayed in the market place. Always it has had enormous influence on the exoteric, or outer religion, of Judaism.

An illuminated manuscript of the Book of Knowledge *by Al-Jazari (c. 1315), featuring the traditional 7-branched menorah.*

Cabala Christianity

Although the Church Fathers of the 1st century CE were undoubtedly Kabbalists, the infighting between different factions of the Roman Church meant that the mystical (Gnostic) elements were largely removed within the first three centuries of its existence. The Renaissance brought a surge of interest in ancient Greek and Hebrew knowledge, and a Christian "Cabala" evolved: a conscious attempt to unite the teachings of Kabbalah, Neoplatonic thought, and those mystical teachings that had survived within the Roman tradition. Despite the antagonism toward the Gnostics, many of the mystical elements that have survived in the Church have their roots in the Mystery tradition.

Qabalah The Western Mystery Tradition

There has always been a hidden, mystical "underbelly" to Western thought. It has shown itself in many forms, in secret or semisecret societies such as the Knights Templar, Freemasons, alchemists, and Rosicrucians. Through them all can be found a common body of knowledge that reaches back into the mists of time. The Order of the Golden Dawn, which was active at the turn of the last century, made the Qabalah a central part of its teaching. This was derived from both Kabbalah and Christian Cabala.

The Rosicrucian symbol of the Golden Dawn, an order that sought to rework the ancient Mysteries. Founded in 1888, it made the Qabalah central to its teachings.

Outline of the book

This book looks at where Kabbalah has come from, how it works, and where it can take us if we use it in our lives. Chapter 1 provides a brief history. Chapter 2 explains the basic ideas of Kabbalah, using the best-known image, "the Tree of Life," and another derived from it, the "Ladder of Light." These two images are the cornerstones of this book. Chapters 3 to 7 are an experiential guide to climbing the Ladder of Light. The final chapter examines some of the areas that Kabbalah has influenced: architecture, astrology, tarot, and psychology.

"St. Paul Preaching," an illuminated manuscript (c. 1526) from the Epistle to the Romans. *During the Renaissance, attempts were made to revive the Kabbalah within the Christian church.*

CHAPTER 1

A History of Kabbalah

Several stories in Jewish folklore describe the mythical origins of the Kabbalah. Traditionally, these teachings were given to humankind by God, lost and then given again through the ages. Of the many mystical Jewish texts written in the last 2,500 years, the earliest recognized now as modern Kabbalah date from medieval times.

God first taught the Kabbalah to the angels, before the world was created. Humankind then received it three times. Adam was first given the teachings by the archangel Raziel, as he and Eve left the Garden of Eden—so that the human race could one day return to Paradise. (The word *Paradise* comes from the Hebrew *Pardes*, meaning orchard.) In time, people lost interest in the "Return to Pardes," becoming more preoccupied with the mundane world, and so the teachings were lost.

The Kabbalah was next given to Abraham as part of the covenant that God made with him. Abraham passed these teachings on, but they were lost again when the Jewish people lived in Egypt. After the Exodus from Egypt, the Kabbalah was returned to God's chosen people. Moses went up the mountain to meet Jehovah twice. The first time he returned with the Ten Commandments—the outer teachings (the number ten plays is central to the Kabbalah). The second time he received the inner teachings.

Moses presenting the Ten Commandments to the Israelites. This was the third (and final) time that God gave the Kabbalah directly to humankind.

Early Religious Texts

The first period to which historians can trace Kabbalah with any certainty is far closer to our era. Following the destruction of the Temple of Jerusalem in 66 CE, and the second Jewish revolt against the Romans in 132 CE, the study of any mystical material was discouraged.

When the Biblical commentaries, known collectively as the Torah, were written down in the 6th century ce, the mystical writings were mostly excluded. Only a few texts, such as the Ma-aseh Merkavah (the Works of the Chariot) and the Ma-aseh Beresheet (the Works of Creation) were documented. These teachings are some way from what we now recognize as Kabbalah.

The Kabbalah Emerges

The earliest documented, definitely Kabbalistic book is the *Sepher Yetzirah,* or *Book of Formation* (sometimes translated as the *Book of Creation*). One tradition says that Abraham wrote down the teachings of the Kabbalah and hid the text in a cave; it was found many centuries later and published as the *Sepher Yetzirah*. Another tradition says that Rabbi Akiva, one of the best-known early Kabbalists, wrote it. He is to be one of the few souls said to have communed with God and come back.

A traditional tale describes four rabbis entering Pardes (Paradise): Ben Azzai, Ben Zoma, Rabbi Akher, and Rabbi Akiva. Ben Azzai gazed and died, because it was his time to leave the world. Ben Zoma gazed and lost his mind, because his mind could not tolerate what he beheld. Rabbi Akher gazed and did not understand what he beheld, and so became an unbeliever. Only Rabbi Akiva entered in peace and left in peace.

This direct experience of God is central to the ideas of Kabbalah. The *Sepher Yetzirah* is the first known text to mention another central concept, that of the thirty-two paths, or stages (the word is *netibuth*, which means both these things and more).

Another enormously influential book is the *Zohar* (*Book of Splendor*). This came to light in the early 14th century via a Spanish Kabbalist named Moses De Leon.

De Leon claimed that he had found the scrolls, and that the original manuscript had been written some twelve hundred years earlier by Rabbi Simon, the foremost disciple of Rabbi Akiva.

Recent research indicates that he probably wrote these scrolls himself. It is a massive work, and consists largely of a commentary on holy scripture, but this is used as a launching pad for some extraordinary explorations of mystical imagery and imagination. It is still used by many Kabbalists today as a fruitful area of research.

The Cabalists of the Christian Renaissance

The Cabala is rightly associated with the foremost Renaissance thinkers and magicians: among them Ramon Lull, Giovanni Pico della Mirandola, John Dee, and Giordano Bruno. Although at the time they were denounced as heretics, they worked, to a greater or lesser extent, to reinvigorate Christianity. They saw no conflict between the teachings of Christianity, of Kabbalah, and of the great Greek Mystery schools, whose work was being rediscovered in Europe at this time.

"The Hermetic Philosophy of Nature," from Opera Chemica *by Ramon Lull (c. 1235–1315), the Spanish theologian and mystic.*

A distinctively Christian Cabala starts with the work of Ramon Lull (1232–1317), during a period when the Muslim Arabs ruled much of Spain. This was a time of religious tolerance, and Muslims, Christians, and Jews lived together in peace. Lull attempted to unify the three religions by developing a mystical and philosophical system containing elements common to all.

Giovanni Pico della Mirandola (1463–94) was enormously influential in establishing ways of thinking that would lead ultimately to the Enlightenment and modern day scientific thought. He studied both Kabbalah and the works of Hermes Trismegistus, a figure now known to be mythical but who was then believed to be the author of many of the teachings that are described as the Mysteries, or the Hermetic Mysteries (Mysteries of Hermes). Mirandola believed that in the Kabbalah he had found the divine revelation which would unify Christianity with all the teachings of the Greek masters, including Plato and Pythagoras. One of his famous 900 theses stated that "no science can better convince us of the divinity of Jesus Christ than magic and the Cabala."

Religious Persecution

Mirandola's most profound insight was that natural and spiritual things are not free, because they cannot change themselves: only humans have the ability to be free. God gave the human race the freedom to change, to make mistakes, and to create new things in the world. This was a radical idea in medieval Europe, where the Church had for centuries controlled and directed humanity's ideas about itself. Unsurprisingly, the Roman Church reacted by rejecting all Kabbalistic/Greek/Hermetic thought, and threatened the individuals who expressed these new ideas with the Inquisition. Although Mirandola, a nobleman, was warned but not questioned by the Inquisition, another influential Cabalist of the following generation, Giordano Bruno (1548–1600), was burned at the stake on account of his beliefs.

Persecuting the individual, however, does not always stop the idea. The most immediate impact of these insights was in the arts. Whereas artists had previously been mere artisans with an ability to translate the Creator's works onto canvas, stone, or paper, they now became artists in the modern sense: creators in their own right, expressing their own truth in their own way.

Italian philosopher Giordano Bruno, Piazza Navona, Rome: his execution inspired the Rosicrucians to struggle against the "tyranny of the Pope."

INTO THE MODERN WORLD

The Englishman John Dee (1527–1608) was a mathematician and geographer. He was the first to apply Euclidean geometry to navigation; made some of the first navigational instruments; and developed the maps that helped to build up the power of the English Navy in the 18th and 19th centuries—all this at a time when the concept of the "scientist" did not even exist, and mathematics was considered to be a branch of magic.

But he is remembered mostly for being the archetypal Renaissance magus, with a deep understanding of the Christian Cabala and the Hermetic tradition. He was Court Astrologer to Elizabeth I, and used astrology to decide the time of her coronation. It seems certain that, through both his contacts and his writings, he lay the foundations of the Rosicrucian movement of the 17th century, which helped to carry the Western Mystery tradition into the modern world.

John Dee (1547–1608)—who was a mathematician and geographer—inspired the Rosicrucian movement.

The Jewish Kabbalists of Safed

With the recapture of Southern Spain by the Catholic Monarchs, Ferdinand and Isabella in the late 15th century, the era of religious tolerance that had been enjoyed by the Jews of Spain came to an end. They were faced with the choice of converting to Catholicism, or facing death or exile. Many traveled to join Jewish communities in Central and Eastern Europe; others chose to leave Europe entirely and went to the Holy Land. One such destination was the town of Safed, in northern Galilee.

An Hasidic Jewish Rabbi sitting on steps in Safed old town, Israel. This town is central to the history of Kabbalah.

The Safed of the 16th and 17th centuries provoked a Golden Age for Kabbalah. Many great Kabbalists worked here, and it was at Safed that the most influential Kabbalist of all time, Isaac Luria, taught his revolutionary system to his disciples.

Moses Cordovero (1522–70) was born in Safed, and was considered a child prodigy: he received a special ordination from the leader of the community, Rabbi Beirav, in 1538 when he was just 16. He wrote many books, the most famous being *Pardes Rimonin* (*The Garden of Pomegranates*). In it he synthesized the teachings of the *Zohar*, which is complex in the extreme, and other Kabbalistic traditions, into a unified whole. This gave the Kabbalah, for the first time, a strong philosophical basis.

The Origins of the Lurianic Kabbalah

Rabbi Isaac Luria (1534–72), also known as the Ari (Lion) of Safed, is acknowledged as the greatest Kabbalist of modern times. Luria was another child prodigy, showing great knowledge of the ancient Hebrew text, the *Talmud,* at the tender age of eight. His family went from Jerusalem to live in Cairo when his father died. Here he continued his studies and, at the age of 17, obtained his own copy of the *Zohar*. This provoked an intense period of meditation and withdrawal from the world, for a total of 15 years—including a two-year period when he was entirely alone in a hut by the Nile, except for traveling home on the Sabbath.

At the end of this period he had a vision telling him to travel to Safed, and he arrived there in 1569. He did not display his knowledge at first, but studied quietly with Cordovero.

It was only when he met up with another Kabbalist, Chaim Vital Calebrese, who recognized his greatness, that his teaching really started. People started to flock to hear him speak. He became known as the "Lion," and the group of young students that grew up around him called themselves the "Lion's Whelps."

But by the end of 1572, Luria was dead. He left no written teachings, but through him, Kabbalah had changed forever. Chaim Vital, who had hardly left his side for the previous two years, and who had become his unofficial scribe, continued to teach Luria's new brand of Kabbalism—without his dedication, Luria's Kabbalism would have been far less influential.

The "Whelps" began to travel abroad, and spread the teachings far and wide. No longer was Kabbalah the province of the learned and the middle-aged, studied only in the synagogue and privately, by flickering candlelight.

Luria had taken the ramblings of the *Zohar* and his own extraordinary insights into the nature of God, and welded them together into a compelling and cohesive mystical cosmology (see pages 32–3). It gave ordinary Jewish people a new hope: after the uncertainties of the expulsion from Spain, many were now awaiting only one thing: the coming of the Messiah.

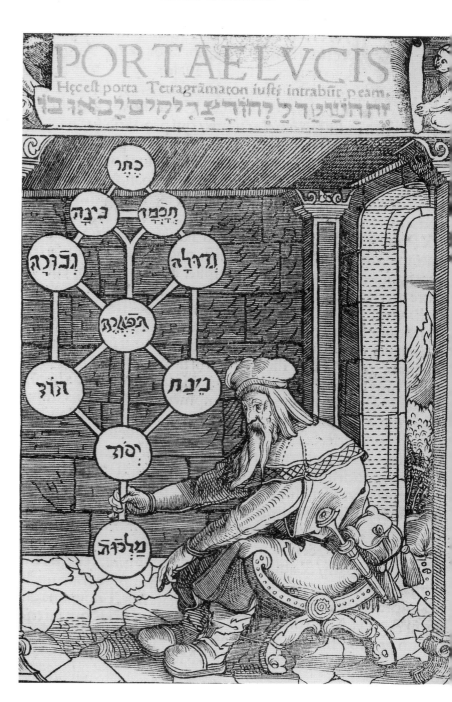

Title picture for the Portae Lucis *(Gates of Light) by Joseph Gikatilla. He probably influenced Moses de Leon, author of the Zohar.*

The Kabbalah in Eastern Europe and Beyond

The next three hundred years were rollercoaster times for the Jewish people. Lurianic Kabbalah was taken after the death of the "Lion" to the many Jewish communities throughout Eastern and Western Europe by his followers, the "Lion's Whelps," and it gained widespread acceptance. But its very success was to become the downfall of Kabbalah in the mainstream Jewish faith.

Above: *Shabbetai Zvi blessing a follower (from* The Counterfeit Messiah *by an English Person of Quality, 18th century).*

Below: *The Ottoman Empire once reached across Europe and the Middle East.*

The Messiah

In 1648—the year that the *Zohar* predicted the Messiah would come—a young man named Shabbetai Zvi from Smyrna in Asia Minor was gathering a small band of followers. A charismatic speaker, well-versed in Lurianic Kabbalah, he and his group were thrown out of their hometown and started traveling throughout the area, slowly attracting followers.

Finally in 1665 came the public announcement at Gaza that Shabbetai was the Messiah, preparing to free God's people. Thousands of Jews believed in him. Word of his existence spread rapidly, and throughout Europe the Jews began preparing for the journey to Palestine, in fulfillment of the Biblical promise that the Messiah would lead them back to the Holy Land.

Palestine was then part of the Ottoman Empire. Shabbetai's secretary Nathan of Gaza wrote letters to the Jewish communities, proclaiming that Shabbetai would ascend to the Ottoman throne with the power of hymns and praises. These letters began to arouse the concern of the authorities.

Finally, in 1666, the Sultan decided he must be stopped. Sabbetai was captured and brought in chains to Constantinople. There, he was given an ultimatum: die, or convert to Islam. He chose to convert, and finally died ten years later, as Aziz Mehmed Effendi, a broken man.

Sabbetai's followers kept their faith; however, the credibility of Kabbalah had been given a terminal blow.

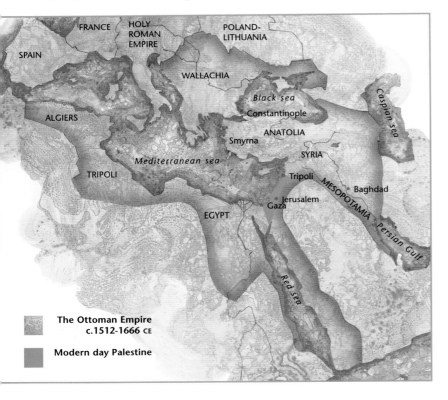

FRANCE   HOLY ROMAN EMPIRE   POLAND-LITHUANIA

SPAIN

WALLACHIA

Black sea

ALGIERS

Constantinople

ANATOLIA

Smyrna

Caspian sea

Mediterranean sea

SYRIA

TRIPOLI

Tripoli

MESOPOTAMIA *Persian Gulf*

Baghdad

Jerusalem

Gaza

EGYPT

Red sea

The Ottoman Empire
c.1512-1666 CE

Modern day Palestine

The Besht

In the 18th century, another Kabbalist took a far less intellectual approach than that of Luria: his students sang, danced, and somersaulted their way to enlightenment. He was uneducated, poor, and virtually unknown up into his mid-30s. Yet his teachings are followed by more Kabbalists in the world today than those of any other master, alive or dead. His name was Israel ben Eliezer, but he became known as the Baal Shem Tov, the "Master of the Good Name," or simply, the Besht.

The Besht was born in the mountains of southern Poland around the turn of the century: his father died when he was very young, and he grew up with hardly any education, being far more interested in exploring the countryside than in being stuck inside, studying.

As a young man he had several lowly jobs, including that of teacher's assistant and watchman, and he developed an interest in Kabbalah. On marrying, he and his wife moved further up into the mountains, where he quarried clay, then took it down into the town to sell for a small sum. All through this time, he studied and developed a direct experience of God in the beauty of his surroundings.

When he was 36, he came down from the mountain and announced that he was a teacher and faith healer. He traveled from town to town, healing the sick and preaching. By all accounts he was a powerful preacher—but a man of few words otherwise. He taught of the joy of God, that he and his works should be celebrated in dance and song.

By the time of his death in 1760, the Besht had laid the firm foundations of the Hassidic movement—a movement that continues to flourish to this day.

The 19th Century

In the wake of the French Revolution, the rapidly changing atmosphere of political reform led to the opening of the ghettos, and the Jews of Europe began to have access to the education that had previously been denied to them. A new generation of cosmopolitan Jews grew up, uninterested in the old ways. The Hassidic Jews were seen as backward and medieval, and so was the Kabbalah. Perhaps the nail in Kabbalah's coffin was the attitude of Heinrich Graetz (1817–91), professor of the Jewish Theological Seminary in Breslau. In his enormously influential book, *History of the Jews*, published in 11 volumes over a 24-year period in the middle of the 19th century, he dismissed the Kabbalah as nonsense, and its teachers as madmen or fools.

It was not until very recently that the Kabbalah was seen as anything other than a backwater by the mainstream Jewish community. These days, with the enormous increase of interest in spiritual matters, the community is starting to reexamine its own mystical heritage.

The Jewish Ghetto in Prague in the early 20th century. At this time, the Kabbalah was rejected as old-fashioned (at best) and as dangerous nonsense (at worst).

The Qabalah in the Western Mystery Tradition

The Western Mystery Tradition outside of Christianity continued largely because of the continual rejection by dogmatic Christian leaders of the possibility of a changed spiritual vision. The Christian Cabalists of the Renaissance thought that the Roman Church would benefit by integrating the ideas of Kabbalah. By the time of the Enlightenment, the foremost thinkers had realized it was possible—even essential—to tread a different path.

A representation of the archetype of the solar system in its most perfect form. *From the* Opus Mago-Cabalisticum *by Georg von Welling (1655–1725).*

The Rosicrucians

In 1614, an extraordinary manuscript was published anonymously at Kassel in Germany, called *Fama Fraternitatis: the Declaration of the Worthy Order of the Rosy Cross.* It described the life and work of one Christian Rosenkreutz, who had founded an occult fraternity that continued to work and study in secret for 120 years after his death. The group were now going public for the first time, following the discovery of Rosenkreutz's tomb. This event was taken to mark the start of a Golden Age in which Rosenkreutz's teachings would usher in a new, more enlightened society of tolerance and goodwill.

The curiosity and interest of the public was aroused, and was further stimulated the following year when the *Confessio Fraternitatis* was published. The year after that, in 1616, *The Chymical Wedding of Christian Rosenkreutz* completed the trilogy. Both added to the mystery of who exactly Christian Rosenkreutz was. Many people tried to contact the Order of the Rosy Cross—the Rosicrucians. If anyone succeeded, there is no record of it. The manuscripts seemed to have appeared from nowhere, and the Order itself seemed now to have disappeared.

All three documents were full of Cabalistic and Hermetic influences, and also showed strong traces of the ideas of John Dee: the *Confessio* is based in part on Dee's magnum opus, *Monas Hieroglyphica*. Modern research now indicates that the documents came from a group based around the University of Tübingen, focused on Johann Valentin Andrea (1586–1654). Christian Rosenkreutz almost certainly never existed.

It seems that the motivation was neither to defraud, nor to gain extra members for any existing organization, but to stimulate debate about a new Christian Golden Age, to be ushered in by enlightened Cabalistic/Hermetic thought. There is no doubt that, in some measure, they succeeded: in the years that followed, a number of groups sprang up, calling themselves "Rosicrucian," teaching the ancient Hermetic Mysteries, and using the imagery and vocabulary of the Rosicrucian documents.

Reverse of a Golden Dawn tarot card showing the "Rosy Cross" of the Rosicrucians. Note the Tree of Life in the center.

THE GOLDEN DAWN

This most famous of occult orders was founded in 1888 by three London Freemasons: Dr. W. R. Woodman, Dr. W. W. Westcott, and S. L. Mathers. They claimed that they had received a dispensation to teach the rituals and techniques of a German Rosicrucian order called "die Goldene Dämmerung"—The Golden Dawn—and produced letters from a Fräulein Sprengel, a Rosicrucian adept and chief of the order, to back up this claim. There are no other traces of either Fräulein Sprengel or a German Golden Dawn, and it seems likely that, like the original Rosicrucian order, ancient origins and titles were invented in order to give credibility to a new working of the ancient Mysteries.

Membership of the Golden Dawn grew quickly—late 19th century London had become an occult center, with the arrival there in 1887 of Madame Blavatsky, founder of the Theosophical Society. Some of the most original thinkers of the day were members, including the poet W. B. Yeats, and the infamous occultist Aleister Crowley.

Cabala (or Qabalah as it was called by the Golden Dawn) was central to the Golden Dawn system. Members were trained in magical techniques—meditation, concentration, ritual, and evocation—to control the outer world as well as learn about the inner one. This is the way in which Qabalah is often thought of today—a long way from the original aim of seeking a direct experience of God.

British occultist Aleister Crowley—when he was about 25 years old—dressed as a Heirophant in the order of the Golden Dawn.

CHAPTER 2

The Tree of Life and the Ladder of Light

This chapter covers the basic concepts of the Kabbalah from Jewish, Christian, and Western Mystery teachings. The essence of the Kabbalah is contained in a single idea—the return to Paradise—and two glyphs—the Tree of Life and the Ladder of Light. These two symbols are the keys to the teachings.

The Return to the Orchard

The central teaching of Kabbalah is that once we lived in communion with God, but that some cosmic catastrophe struck, and we were cast out of that marvellous state—and yearn to return. All the exercises and study of Kabbalah have one single aim: to return us to the paradise from whence we came. In Christian tradition, this blissful state is known as the Garden of Eden. In Kabbalistic/Judaic tradition, the same place is also identified with the Orchard (Pardes) that Rabbi Akiva and his colleagues visited. This journey represents the direct experience of God, which is central to the teachings of Kabbalah.

Paradise, to which we long to return—a detail from The Garden of Earthly Delights *by Hieronymus Bosch (c.1450–1516).*

The Central Symbols and Concepts of the Kabbalah

The Tree of Life can be likened to a map. The power of this symbol is its flexibility: it teaches on many different levels. It can give us insight into the world we live in, and into our psychological make-up. It describes how our minds work, and reveals a profound understanding of our essence, our spirit.

The tree is quite a well-known symbol—its outline even appeared as a crop circle in England in the mid-1990s. It is this glyph, and another derived from it, called the Ladder of Light, that will provide the cornerstones of this book.

The basic building blocks of the Tree of Life are called the ten *sephiroth* (singular *sephira*). This is a Hebrew word meaning "enumeration." The Ladder of Light is an extension of the Tree of Life, and although it might look more complicated, it shows some Kabbalistic principles more clearly. It is made up of interpenetrating trees, and has 32 stages, a concept which comes from the Hebrew word *netibuth*, meaning path, way, or stage.

This chapter examines the basic concepts required to understand the Tree of Life and the Ladder of Light, and focuses on the process of creation: that is, the journey down the tree or ladder, from the Creator at the top to the Created at the bottom. Subsequent chapters will examine the path of return.

The Tree of Life is central to the teachings of the Kabbalah. It offers insights into the world around us and the world within us. (Gustav Klimt, 1862–1918.)

The Tree of Life The Supernals

The supernal (celestial) sephiroth express concepts on an archetypal level, as general principles. They describe what is indescribable, except by using approximation and example. There are three supernal sephiroth and they sit at the top of the Tree of Life.

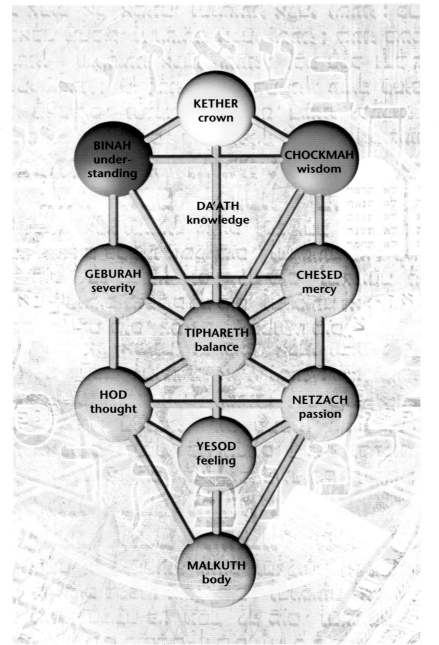

They are *Kether* (pronounced "ketta") meaning Crown, *Chockmah* (pronounced "hockma," with a Scottish "ch" as in "loch") which means Wisdom, and *Binah* (pronounced "beena") meaning Understanding. These three form the "supernal triangle," and they represent great archetypal energies rather than specific qualities. It is not always possible to experience these three directly.

Sephira 1 Kether, the Crown
When the Tree of Life is laid out on the figure of a human, Kether lies just above the head.

A crown is not part of a king, but a king cannot rule without it. So it is with Kether: nothing can "be" without it, yet it is above and beyond all things. It is "no-thing." And it is everything. Kether can be likened to God, who simply is, without needing to relate to anything else. It is the ultimate source, described by some as the Mind of God—and to humans the mind of God can only be unknowable.

Kether might be likened to the time before the "Big Bang" of modern-day physics, the original source of the universe. Physicists can calculate what happened immediately—micro- or even pico-seconds—after the Big Bang, but there are no formulae that can describe what actually occurred at the moment of the Big Bang itself. The experience of Kether is union with God.

CHOCKMAH

Sephira 2 Chockmah, Wisdom

If Kether is "no-thing," then Chockmah is "something." Chockmah is the archetypal masculine or yang principle, the creative force that pours itself into existence: the results of the Big Bang. This outpouring contains all things, hence the name of Wisdom, which contains everything.

When written in Hebrew, the first letter of the word "Hockma" is a Yod. This letter represents an initiatory, fecundating power. Any rushing, unstoppable force has the quality of Chockmah behind it. It is important to remember that this is only incidentally linked to men or male sexuality. Women are just as able to express this principle as men, as it is fundamental to life.

Chockmah happens when God decides to take time for self-reflection: it is the act of God moving to a place where he can experience himself. The quality or virtue of Chockmah is devotion.

BINAH

Sephira 3 Binah, Understanding

Just as Chockmah is the primordial masculine, Binah is the primordial feminine, or yin principle. Extending the idea of the Big Bang, theoretical physicists speculate about a point at which the outrushing forces are overcome by gravity and the universe starts to fall in on itself again. This picture suggests a limit: the limit of expansion is reached.

Binah defines this limit: it takes the force of Chockmah and forms it. God here molds herself, limits her self-expression. If God moves out to experience herself, and just keeps going, she can learn nothing. The quality of limitation is required to bring back the parts of herself she has sent out. The quality or virtue of Binah is silence.

The Big Bang—when the universe was created. If Kether is the nothing that preceded this, Chockmah is the act of creation and Binah the limit that defines this.

THE SUPERNAL TRIAD

Another way of thinking about the supernal triad is to compare it to the way that color is created from light.

1. Kether is the light source.
2. Chockmah is the focused beam that streams out from the light source.
3. Binah is the prism through which the light is scattered.

None of these three has color in itself, yet together they produce the rainbow of seven colors, representing the remaining seven sephiroth of the Tree of Life.

Tree of Life Chesed, Geburah, and Tiphareth

The first three sephiroth are totally archetypal: they do not have any link with reality as it is experienced. The next three sephiroth are reflections of the first, on a lower level. They express the same energies as the supernal triad, now on a closer-to-human level—but still as general principles, rather than as specific qualities.

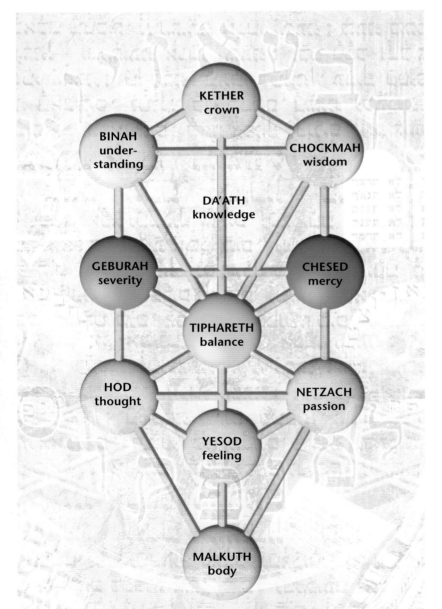

The Abyss

The third sephira, Binah, defines the end of the purely archetypal realm and the beginnings of form. At this point, the Tree of Life shows a gap: there is a space between the first three sephiroth and the second triad. This gap is called the Abyss.

When crossing the Abyss from above, we leave the "heavenly" realms of God and start on a more concrete experience. We move from being to doing, or from theory to practice. On a human level, just imagine if there was no abyss between thinking a thought and acting it out—what chaos there would be in the world!

Sephira 4 Chesed, Mercy

The fourth sephiroth is the first on "our" side of the Abyss: it is here that we can have a first direct experience of God. *Chesed* (pronounced "hesed," with a Scottish "ch" as in "loch"), meaning mercy, also translates as compassion, and it represents the principles of generosity—the loving, giving God—and of obedience.

As the first sephira below the Abyss, Chesed also represents the level of the "Inner Plane Adepts": individuals who no longer need to incarnate on earth, and who could cross the Abyss and move on to the next stage of their evolution. Instead, they have

In Hinduism the concepts of conscience and balance are fused in the term "Karma"—in Kabalah, Geburah expresses a very similar concept.

Geburah is associated with Mars, the Roman God of War.

On an inner level, Geburah relates to conscience: it represents the concept that is expressed by the Hindu term "Karma." Every action has a consequence, every action in one direction will have an equal and opposite action in the other.

If we were conscious at the Geburrhic level, we would have the same level of awareness that is reported occasionally by those who have a near-death experience, where life flashes before our eyes at the moment of death and every action is seen for exactly what it is—for good or ill.

This is what the Ancient Egyptians called The Hall of the 42 Assessors: in this situation, people's deeds are weighed in the balance, and the verdict on their life is given—impartial justice, firm but fair.

Geburah gives us the strength to face things that are wrong, and the ability to change them. An imbalance may lead to cowardice, fear, and violence.

chosen to stay in contact with people still incarnated in the physical realm, to offer help and guidance to all who follow a spiritual path.

In Chesed we find the qualities of giving others and ourselves the benefit of the doubt, of forgiveness, generosity, and an optimistic outlook. An imbalance may lead to overindulgence and hypocrisy.

Sephira 5 Geburah, Severity

GEBURAH

The fourth and fifth sephira working together show one really important principle of Kabbalah: balance. Where Chesed is expansion, *Geburah* (pronounced "geboora") is limitation. The two sephiroth will always work together to find the middle way. Geburah is, for example, the surgeon's scalpel, cutting away at the excess growth of cancer cells in the body, or the soldier fighting to protect his homeland from an invading army's expansion—

Sephira 6 Tiphareth, Balance

TIPHARETH

Tiphareth (pronounced "tifareth") is at the center of the Tree of Life, hence the meaning of its name: balance. Within any tree, Tiphareth represents the inner core and the place where consciousness sits most readily. The sun is the Tiphareth of our solar system; in the body Tiphareth is placed at the solar plexus, the center of balance, from which, according to many schools of martial arts, an enormous amount of physical energy can emanate. This is also the place of the higher self, or guardian angel, and of the inner child.

Tiphareth represents the qualities of health, balance, and courage. An imbalance may lead to pride and ego-inflation.

At the Old Bailey law courts in London, England, the statue of Justice shows her holding the scales of balance, on which evidence is weighed.

Tree of Life Netzach, Hod, Yesod, and Malkuth

The lower four sephiroth consist of the third triad and the tenth and final sephira, Malkuth. The third triad expresses the archetypal energies of the first in a concrete, practical way: it is at this level that our day-to-day consciousness is focused. Malkuth represents the place where we experience all the energies of the higher sephiroth.

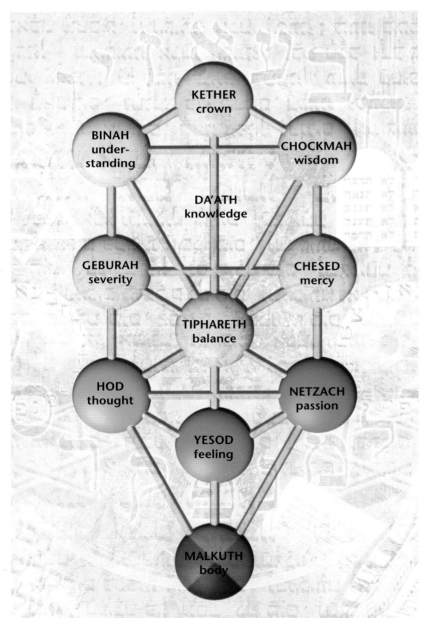

The Veil

Below Chesed, Geburah, and Tiphareth there is another division, known in the Western tradition as the Veil. This marks the end of a realm that is still rather beyond our normal consciousness: the sephiroth between the Abyss and the Veil still describe principles rather than realities.

Below the Veil comes the lower triad of Netzach, Hod, and Yesod, and then finally Malkuth. These sephiroth describe far more familiar energies, and our normal, everyday consciousness is bounded by the triangle formed at the bottom of the Tree of Life, centered on Yesod.

Sephira 7 Netzach, Passion

Netzach (again pronounced with a soft Scottish "ch") is represented in the skies by the planet Venus, the beautiful evening star, and named after the Roman Goddess of Love. This sephira represents the passion and energy of the creative process, both in humanity and in nature. The most important thing for Netzach is relationships and creativity, of all types and at all levels. Whether it is physical sex, the gardener cultivating plants, or the artist creating his or her magnum opus—all of these express the energy of Netzach. An imbalance of Netzach may lead to the misuse of relationships or creativity, expressed as an abuse of sexual energy, or such actions as stealing the fruits of another's work.

Sephira 8 Hod, Thought

The sephira *Hod* is currently very strong in the Western world. It represents the realm of thought: all communication and technology that enable communication, from writing to mobile phones. The planet Mercury, named for the Roman messenger of the Gods, represents Hod in the solar system. Hermes (the Greek equivalent) was the only Olympian God allowed to enter the realm of Hades, the Underworld. This aspect of Hod has come to the fore in the last 100 years with the rise of psychoanalysis, which illuminates the unconscious mind. Hod's quality is truthfulness. An imbalance may lead to dishonesty.

Sephira 9 Yesod, Feeling

The experience of *Yesod* is about a non-rational way of being; of knowing about something as a "gut feeling." For many in the West such experience has been pushed into the subconscious in the face of Hod-dominated intellectualism. Yesod represents a level of reality just above the physical, known as the astral plane of being. It is at Yesod that imagination and dreams have reality, in the plastic forms of the "Treasure House of Images"—another name for this sephira. All created things must pass through Yesod before being actualized on the physical plane. For this reason, Yesod is also known as the Foundation. This sephira corresponds in the physical body to the sexual organs, and has a lot to do with the application of energy (physical and sexual) in the last sephira, Malkuth.

Yesod is the place of cycles and rhythm, and is linked to femininity, as well as to the moon and its daily and monthly cycles. Yesod's quality is independence, of mind and of action. An imbalance may lead to idleness and dependence on others.

Sephira 10 Malkuth, Body

The word *Malkuth* comes from the Hebrew *mal*, meaning royal, and *kuth*, meaning vulva: this is the Gate of Manifestation we all pass through to arrive on Earth. It can also be translated as 'kingdom.'

Another Hebrew term for this sephira is Shekhinah, the bride of the Messiah. In some Kabbalistic traditions, it is the Shekhinah, the female principle, that has been cast out from Heaven. The path of Kabbalah is then to reunite the Shekhinah and the Messiah in ourselves.

The quality associated with Malkuth is discrimination. An imbalance may lead to materialism, narrow-mindedness, and avarice: the obsession with and desire for material possessions.

Malkuth is the place of outer forms, of physical existence. Hence, in the individual, it is the body, where personal energies manifest, and in the outer world, it is the kingdom, where the commands of the crown (kether) are carried out. This physical existence is represented by the four elements of Earth, Water, Air, and Fire, which symbolically make up all matter.

As a method of communication, the cellular phone is governed by Hod, the sephira of thought. Hod currently dominates the Western world.

Repentant prostitute Mary Magdalene represents Shekhinah, the bride of the Messiah—the female principle cast out from Heaven.

The *Sepher Yetzirah*

Almost all Rabbinical Kabbalah uses what are known as Yetziratic teachings, which have become the basis of many Christian and Western Mystery Kabbalistic teachings over the past thousand years. The teachings are taken from the Sepher Yetzirah (Book of Formation), a small book—about the same size as the Tao Te Ching—with an influence out of all proportion to its size. The appearance of the Sepher Yetzirah marked a significant change in direction for the Kabbalistic tradition, because it introduced several concepts that became central to Kabbalah.

Rabbi Akiva, the mystic and scholar, was thought to have written the Book of Formation, *a central work in Kabbalistic thought. (Woodcut from Haggadah, Italy, 16th century.)*

The *Sepher Yetzirah* describes a total of 32 intelligences or emanations that make up the body and mind of God. These consist of the numbers 1 to 10, and the 22 letters of the Hebrew alphabet. The imagery draws on the teachings known as the *Merkavah*, based on the Biblical prophet Ezekiel's vision of a chariot.

There are also two commentaries, whose antiquity is uncertain: they can only be traced with any certainty to 17th-century publications of the *Sepher Yetzirah*.

They are:

• The 50 Gates of Intelligence, which list the route of ascent from Hyle (Chaos), through the mineral, vegetable, and animal kingdoms, humanity, the planets, and the orders of angels to God.

• The 32 Stages of Wisdom, which describe the intelligences or emanations that make up the body and mind of God, with a few lines describing the quality of each. The image of the Tree of Life owes much of its current form—10 spheres and 22 paths—to this text.

The Origins of the Book of Formation

Tradition says that the work goes back to the patriarch Abraham, or at least to the saintly Rabbi Akiva of the 1st century CE, but the most recent research indicates that it was written no earlier than the 5th century CE. Various linguistic and contextual clues have linked it to an unlikely, but intriguing source.

The last of the great Neoplatonic teachers was Proclus Diadochus (410–85 CE). He studied with the philosopher Plutarch at Plato's Academy in Athens. Proclus was an initiate of the Greek Mystery schools, and much of his work is clearly based on these ancient teachings. There are many similarities between the teachings of Proclus and the *Sepher Yetzirah*. Among them are the concepts of emanation, development from a trinity, and *henad*, a word meaning enumeration—rather like sephira.

In past times it was common practice to write a book or essay on a particular subject and publish it using the name of a famous dead person who was known as an expert on that subject—the impact of the book would then be that much greater. It is now believed by some Biblical scholars that many of the Epistles, and all of the Gospels in the New Testament, were written in this way. It has been suggested that the similarity between the *Sepher Yetzirah* and Proclus's teachings came about through a student of Proclus presenting the Mystery teaching in a form acceptable to anyone with knowledge of the Jewish mystical tradition. It is well known that many Mystery cults started through initiates of the Mystery schools adapting what they had learned to their own native traditions. A recent book—*The Jesus Mysteries* by Timothy Freke and Peter Gandy, 1999—expounds the theory that Paul of Tarsus—himself an initiate of the Greek Mystery schools—started a Mystery cult for Jews that was taken up by non-Jews and was ultimately to become Christianity.

The Mixing of Traditions

There is another fascinating aspect of this. The early Christian mystical author Dionysius the Areopagite wrote two influential treatises, *The Celestial Hierarchies* and *Mystical Theology*. This Dionysius was a convert of St. Paul in the 1st century. But Christian historians, after textual analysis and other studies, are now certain that he is not the author. It seems more likely a student of Proclus Diadochus wrote the books in the 6th century. If true, this means that significant portions of Jewish and Christian mysticism have their origins in a virtually unknown pagan philosopher of the 5th century, and their roots in the Greek Mystery schools, whose the origins go back to ancient Egypt and beyond.

The School of Athens *by Raphael (1483–1520). It was here that Proclus and Plutarch studied and taught.*

Dionysius the Areopagite was a Christian mystical author.

Movement on the Tree of Life

It is easy to think of the Tree of Life as a static symbol. The reality is that any process, any act of creation, any growing organism can be represented on a tree: it is effectively a universal wiring diagram, and once applied to a system, the patterns of energy can be seen to flow around it constantly. With the sephiroth we have the fixed points of the system. Dependent on the system, they can represent any number of things. In a physical body, they represent the outer physiology (Malkuth), through the nervous system (Hod), and seat of consciousness (Tiphareth), to the ideal, archetypal body (Kether). This section examines some of the ways in which change and movement is represented on the tree.

The Tree of Knowledge has roots in the worlds of light and dark. Sephiroth Tree: from the Studium Universale *by the Lutheran minister Valentin Weigel.*

The Paths

If the sephiroth represent different states of consciousness, the paths represent the change of consciousness that occurs when moving between them.

There are 22 paths, corresponding to the 22 letters of the Hebrew alphabet. Most systems of Kabbalah attribute the 10 sephiroth and 22 paths to the 32 Stages of Wisdom. The Golden Dawn, like the Christian Cabalists before them, established correspondences between the paths and the Hebrew letters, as well as the 22 Tarot trumps, the astrological signs, the planets, animals, herbs, and a whole host of other symbols.

This work gives a rich source of imagery that can be used when imagining how consciousness changes when moving from one sephira to another. This technique, known as pathworking, is an important component of the teachings of the contemporary Western Mystery Tradition.

The Lightning Flash

This follows the path of the sephiroth down the Tree of Life: the order in which they are described on pages 20–25. This sequence describes the process of creation, from the Creator in Kether to the Created in Malkuth.

In all places it travels along paths, except where it crosses the Abyss. At this point the Creator has to have an intense focus on the act of creation: the leap from the abstract to the manifest is not an easy one to make.

The Energetic Triangles

The paths on the tree make many triangles. Each triangular path represents the flow of energy between the three Sephiroth involved. Much can be learned and understood by looking at the triangles— consider the following examples:

Malkuth—Yesod—Hod This triangle represents the process of learning by rote: impressions are received in Malkuth, visualized in Yesod, and analyzed in Hod. The lesson is fed back to Yesod, where it becomes a memory. The energy then moves down again to receive more sensory information.

Malkuth—Yesod—Netzach This triangle is to do with learning by doing—the urge to action is generated in Netzach and moves down to Malkuth. The results of the action are then visualized in Yesod and fed back to Netzach for further action.

Hod—Geburah—Tiphareth This triangle represents self-discipline. For example, a friend asks you out for a meal tonight. Hod reacts by thinking what a good thing that would be to do. The energy of the thought moves up to Geburah, where the realization of having

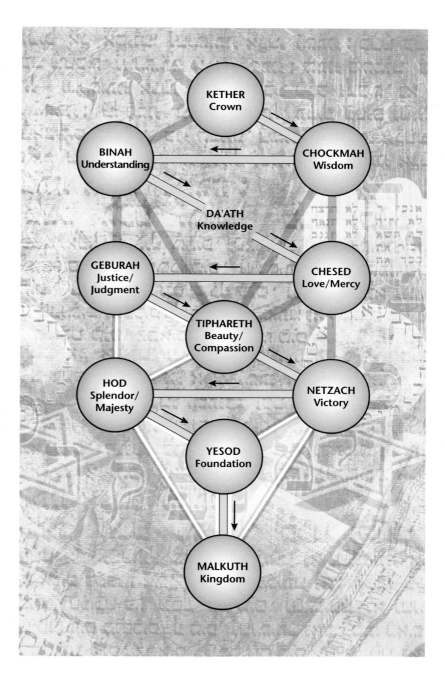

to work late this evening arises. The information is fed back to the Self in Tiphareth, where it is considered, and the offer of the meal declined.

The Lightning Flash moves down the Tree of Life. (Some of the energetic triangles are shown here in white.)

Patterns of the Tree of Life

The patterns described in this section complete this extremely brief outline of the main features of the Tree of Life. These particular patterns are also significant because they form the basis of ideas by which the Tree of Life is transformed into the Ladder of Light, on which the rest of this book is based.

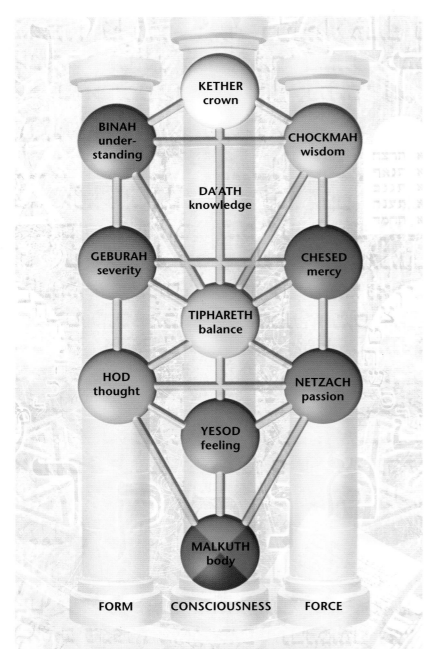

FORM   CONSCIOUSNESS   FORCE

Da'ath—the sephira that is not there

There have been many conjectures about the space in the Abyss a sephira could occupy: it has been given the name *Da'ath* (pronounced as in Daath Vader from the movie *Star Wars*), which means knowledge.

When approaching the Abyss from below, the experience is one of approaching the unknown. The best way to cross the unknown is by gaining knowledge of it. This is the purpose of Da'ath. Its symbol is an empty room. It can be seen as an image of Kether, which is otherwise totally unreachable. On the negative side, Da'ath has also been called the False Head: it is easy to think that knowledge is the Crown (Kether), the goal to reach. It is not. Any attempt to stay here—with information but no insight (knowledge without wisdom and understanding)—will fail: we fall into the Abyss of ignorance. Only once the Abyss has been crossed does Da'ath change into the foundation stone for the next step on the path. Da'ath hides a great secret. The secret is that day by day, in facing our own Abyss, and through faith crossing it, we transform Knowledge into something far more profound, and move our life onward, to another level.

The Pillars

The sephiroth on the Tree of Life form three columns, or pillars. The middle pillar consists of

Malkuth at the base, and Yesod, Tiphareth, and Kether, passing through Da'ath between Tiphareth and Kether. This is called the pillar of consciousness.

The right-hand pillar starts from the top with Chockmah, with Chesed at the center, and Netzach at the base. This is the pillar of force. All the sephiroth on this side are to do with movement, expansion, and energy.

The left-hand pillar starts from the top with Binah, with Geburah at the center, and Hod at the base. This is the pillar of form. All the sephiroth on this side are to do with restriction, contraction, and matter.

Each pair of sephiroth on each level can balance each other: it is the corresponding sephira on the middle pillar which pivots that balance, by being conscious of the adjustment that is required.

The Caduceus

Asclepius, the Greek God of Healing, owned the caduceus, so it is well known as the symbol of medicine. However, it has had other owners. Hermes, the Greek messenger god, and Thoth, the Egyptian god of the underworld, both gods of the Mysteries, possessed such staffs, wrapped around with intertwining snakes.

The Qabalah adopted the caduceus, and placed it over the Tree of Life. It is said to represent the three paths of access to the spirit: the staff itself represents the middle way, the purple ray that leads most directly straight up to the top. This is the path of Love, of the mystic, the rabbi, and the priesthood, where God is found in devotion.

The orange snake curling to the right at the bottom, which passes through Hod, is known as the Hermetic Way, and the orange ray. This is the path

of the mind: the intellectual, analyzing way, where God is found in analysis and comprehension. The green snake curling to the left, which passes through Netzach, indicates the path of the green ray, and the Orphic Way. This is the path of nature, where God is found in ecstasy and action.

The Upper and Lower Countenances

The countenances, or faces, of the tree are the two large quadrilaterals which meet at Tiphareth. The upper face is centered on Da'ath and consists of Kether, Chockmah, Tiphareth, and Binah. It represents God. The lower face is centered on Yesod and is made up of Tiphareth, Netzach, Malkuth, and Hod. It represents humanity.

Points on the caduceus are associated with points on the Tree of Life—the numbers shown here correspond to the ten sephiroth as follows:

1 = Kether
2 = Chockmah
3 = Binah
4 = Chesed
5 = Geburah
6 = Tiphareth
7 = Netzach
8 = Hod
9 = Yesod
10 = Malkuth

Lurianic Kabbalah

Isaac Luria's work was based on his intense study of the Zohar (see pages 12–13). The Zohar is vast and, at times, deliberately obscure, but Luria's vision brought the many tangled strands together to form a comprehensive cosmology, which for the first time gave the Kabbalah a proper mystical framework.

Sephiroth trees corresponding to descriptions by Isaac Luria. From Scroll of Trees, *Poland, 19th century. Alfred Cohen Collection.*

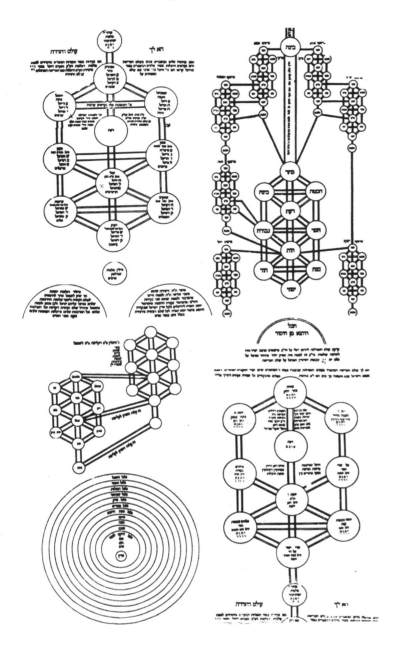

Luria's most profound insight is that God, the Creator, is himself evolving—via the process of creation. And we, his creations, are an important part of the process of His evolution. The part of God that is the Creator is called Adam Kadmon, the Archetypal Man. Luria saw creation as a balance between the forces of contraction and the forces of expansion and described its three phases.

Phase One: Tzimtzum, *or Limitation*

If God is omniscient and omnipotent, there is "no-where" for him to create anything that is not him. So before creation starts, God has to limit himself: to withdraw from a "where," so that creation can occur. In this "where" is created a world known as *Nekudot*, or world of points. This world consists of ten lights, but not in the form of the Tree, because these lights have no relationship to each other—they just float freely.

Phase Two: Sheviret HaKelim, *or Breaking of the Vessels*

The Creator now pours his creative forces in an expansive wave into the lights, or sephiroth. However, the sephiroths' nature is that of *Din*, meaning limitation, and they cannot carry the force of the Creator's light, so they shatter and spill the sparks of light. The first three sephiroth are the strongest, and they do not shatter as much as the other seven. Instead they drop out of Nekudot, creating a lower world as they fall. The last sephira, Malkuth, is also strong. As a result, it does not shatter, but it falls further than any of the others, creating the lowest world of all. The space through which the lower seven sephiroth and the sparks of light fall is the Abyss.

Phase Three: Tikkum, or Reparation

The sparks of the Creator's light reside in humanity: one spark sits in each of us. Ultimately, we all need to return to the Creator to make good the damage. To start this process of reparation, four worlds are formed by the shattered sephiroth, which relate to each other through the paths on the Tree of Life.

There are two pairs of worlds, *Abba* and *Ima*—Father and Mother—and *Ze'er Anpin* and *Nukva*. Father and Mother represent the archetypal male/female energies and other binary oppositions, such as positive and negative, and black and white. These polarities are also known as Yin and Yang in Taoist traditions. The Ze'er Anpin and Nukva are reflections in the lower world of Abba and Ima, and are also known as "The Messiah" and "The Shekhinah."

Tikkum is ongoing. To repair the damage, the Shekhinah and the Messiah need to be reunited, so they can return together to the Creator. This reunion is one objective of the individual Kabbalist's spiritual practice: by working toward our own Pardes, we are bringing closer the day when the Messiah and his bride, the Shekhinah, will be reunited. It is this vision of Tikkum that made the Israelites God's "chosen people." Through the revelations of Moses, God chose them to do this work as a nation, rather than as individuals.

THE FEMININE ASPECT

To the average man, either Jew or Christian, the idea of an aspect of God being female was—maybe still is—blasphemous. For this reason, if for no other, the study of Kabbalah was limited by the Rabbis to those family men who were established "pillars of society." It was considered they would not become unbalanced by the use of such sexual imagery!

Many esoteric and religious traditions use sexual imagery to describe spiritual truths—the Hindu Shiva and his consort Parvati.

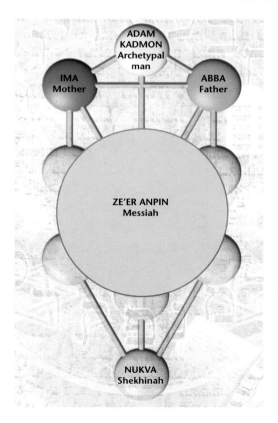

On the Tree of Life, Adam Kadmon appears in Kether (negative existence); Father appears in Chockmah; Mother appears in Binah; Messiah appears in Chesed to Yesod; and Shekhinah appears in Malkuth.

ADAM KADMON
Archetypal man

IMA
Mother

ABBA
Father

ZE'ER ANPIN
Messiah

NUKVA
Shekhinah

The Ladder of Light Adam Kadmon and the Four Worlds

The diagram known as the Ladder of Light pulls the teachings of Lurianic Kabbalah into a single glyph. It derives from the Tree of Life, but instead of one tree, there are now five trees, each interpenetrating the other. This ladder was first alluded to in the Old Testament in the dream of the patriarch Jacob, who saw angels ascending to heaven and descending to earth on a fiery ladder.

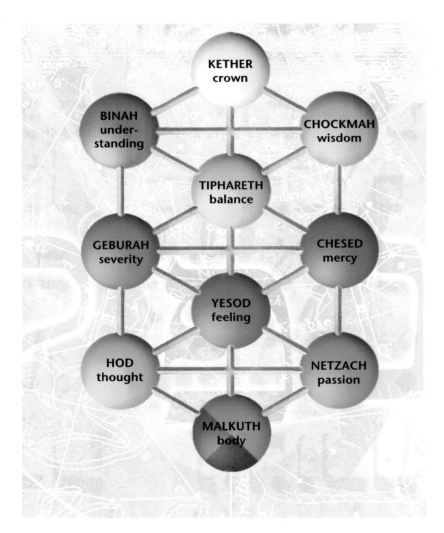

Adam Kadmon

The Creator part of God is Adam Kadmon and he made us in his image. He therefore has the same form as us, but because the Creator's vessels did not break and fall, he is represented by the Perfect Tree, and the 22 paths linking the sephiroth are perfectly symmetrical (see figure, left). Unlike the tree we have been studying so far, the perfect Kadmon Tree has 10 sephiroth, with no inconvenient gaps.

This Kadmon Tree can be found at the top of the glyph known as the Ladder of Light (see opposite). This glyph has 32 stages, as described by the *Sepher Yetzirah*, and 10 sephiroth—not nine or eleven (the large circles joining the paths to each other)—and it also shows both the perfect Kadmon Tree and four imperfect Trees of Life in each of the four worlds.

It is worth noting that the word "stage" represents the Hebrew word *netibuth*, meaning track, path, or way. It has been translated as "stage" in order to distinguish it from the "paths" that link the sephiroth.

The Perfect Tree is that of Adam Kadmon, the creator part of God. This tree has 22 symmetrical paths linking the sephiroth.

THE FOUR WORLDS

The Ladder of Light shows the journey upward through the imperfect worlds of Assiah, Yetzirah, Briah, and Atziluth to reach the perfect Kadmon tree. Each of the four worlds relates to a particular type of consciousness:

Assiah represents the physical world

Yetzirah represents the psychological world

Briah represents the mental world

Atziluth represents the spiritual world

The world of Adam Kadmon represents the world of God

Each world has a complete Tree, going from Malkuth to Kether. And the trees interpenetrate each other:

- The lower face of Assiah, the physical world, is of itself.
- The lower face of Yetzirah, the psychological world, interpenetrates the upper face of Assiah.
- The lower face of Briah, the mental world, interpenetrates the upper face of Yetzirah.
- The lower face of Atziluth, the spiritual world, interpenetrates the upper face of Briah.
- The upper face of Atziluth, the spiritual world, interpenetrates the lowest seven sephiroth of the Kadmon Tree.

The Experience of the Abyss in the World Trees

The psychologist Carl Gustav Jung did an enormous amount of research into the similarities between modern psychology and the ancient Mystery traditions. He said that problems which we encounter on our path of spiritual growth "are not solved, they are transcended." So it is with the experience of the Abyss as we move up through the four worlds to the world of Adam Kadmon.

How often in our lives have we faced a situation that seemed totally daunting and impossible to cope with? Yet a day, a month, a year later, we suddenly realize that we did pass through the crisis, because something shifted somewhere, and we are now moving on.

Moving up through each of the world trees, we experience the lower seven sephiroth, from Malkuth

to Chesed. At Chesed we reach the Abyss. We cannot cross to the supernals of the tree without external help. This help comes from the interpenetration of the tree above—we shift consciousness into the Malkuth of a tree where the Abyss does not yet exist.

By then moving up the tree of the higher world, we find that we have actually crossed the Abyss of the lower world: the Da'ath of the original world is now the Yesod of the one above.

The knowledge (Da'ath) of a lower world is simply the foundations (Yesod) on which we can build the next step on the journey back to Pardes, the Orchard.

The last two sections in this chapter take a look at Assiah, Yetzirah, Briah, and Atziluth, representing the physical, psychological, mental, and spiritual worlds.

Atziluth: The Gods, and **Briah:** The Archangels

Atziluth (the spiritual world) and Briah (the mental world) are the place of Abba and Ima, the archetypal male and female. These are also the worlds of energy and of pattern. They correspond, on a single Tree of Life, to the archetypal, supernal sephiroth above the Abyss. They make up the top half of the Ladder of Light.

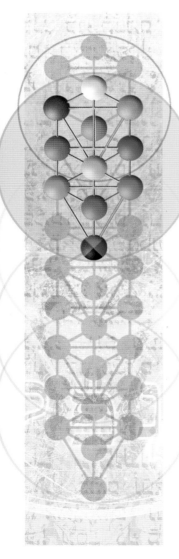

Atziluth, World of Fire and Insight The Gods
Atziluth is the world closest to the world of the Creator, Adam Kadmon. Atziluth means "emanation," implying an emergence from nothing. It is the process by which nothing becomes something, but it is before creation as such, which belongs to the next world, Briah. It is pure energy, with no form at all.

The word "gods" conjures up any number of images for us. All native traditions have a pantheon of gods, and we will all have heard of one or more of the members of other cultures' heavens. For the Kabbalist, the term "gods" means something slightly different. It means the form in which the One God manifests in each of the sephiroth: each god is an emanation from Adam Kadmon, an aspect of Him. As such, these gods are immensely significant as the originators of everything we experience in our lives.

The level on which gods function is beyond both emotion and thought, but it is not beyond consciousness. There is a faculty that we all have which might be called a religious or spiritual sense. It is the "knowingness" we sometimes get about someone or something which is beyond all logic, contradicting any superficial impressions about it or them. It could also be characterized as insight or intuition.

This faculty is associated with the element fire. Its mastery symbolizes humanity's advance over other animals: it is the spark of divine fire within each of us that calls us out of ourselves, toward the light. Atziluth is the world of Abba, the Father, and is paired with Briah, the world of Ima, the Mother.

Fire is associated with Atziluth, the world of insight, which is close to the world of the Creator. Within each of us is a spark of divine fire calling us toward him.

The world of Air, Briah, is the world of creative thought. Carried by the winds, our minds move from one thought to another.

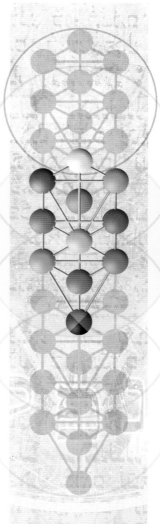

Briah, World of Air and Knowledge
The Archangels

If Atziluth acts as the initial energy, the energy of conception, Briah applies creativity to that energy, and starts to build a pattern around which the Atziluthic energies may flow. The Jewish and Christian Kabbalists characterize this process in terms of beings called archangels. As with the Atziluthic gods, there is very little connection between the normal picture we have of archangels, and the Kabbalistic notion.

There is one archangel for each of the sephiroth, which channels the energies around the appropriate patterns. The Archangels act like generals, with wisdom and understanding (Chockmah and Binah), and plan the actions that their troops, the angels, will take in the next world down.

Briah is the realm of thought. Not the thought of everyday consciousness, but the kind of creative, imaginative thought that ultimately brings new forms into the world. Thought is associated with the element of air: they both have a quality of clarity. The wind gusts and changes, just as the mind jumps from one thought to another.

We may have a sudden flash of inspiration, a bolt out of the blue. In order to create with it, it needs to be put into a pattern, a plan, a context. Without the directing of the world of Briah, the Atziluthic energy stays as that: undifferentiated and shapeless. When working with direction, our thoughts are functioning at their best.

If Atziluth is the spark of God that makes us reach beyond ourselves, Briah is the breath of God that makes us human. Eating the fruit from the Tree of Knowledge (of good and evil) happens in Briah—another title for Briah is Paradise. Having eaten, we lose our innocence: we start to experience polarity, and have to fall into the lower worlds in order to experience and fully integrate this knowledge into ourselves. Like a womb, Briah provides the space in which the formative forces of Yetzirah may function.

Yetzirah: The Angels, and Assiah: The Planets

Yetzirah (the psychological world) and Assiah (the physical world) are the place of Ze'er Anpin and Nukyam, the Messiah and the Shekhinah. Here the work of humanity—the divine marriage of these two—takes place, in the worlds of force and form. They make up the bottom half of the Ladder of Light.

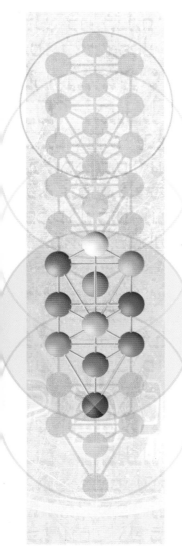

Yetzirah, World of Water and Consciousness
The Angels

Yetzirah, the world of emotion, is represented by the element water. The qualities of water are quite familiar, and are often used to describe emotional states: "still waters run deep," "overflowing with joy," "head swimming with excitement"—and there are many others. Tears often accompany deeply emotional experiences. Other qualities of water describe Yetzirah rather well. It can take on any shape, is often difficult to contain, and can be enormously powerful.

Angels are the beings that operate in Yetzirah. Like the gods and the archangels, the angels are divided into ten different classifications, one for each sephira. Their task is to take the archetypes, energies, and patterns of the higher worlds and use them to form the lower world of Assiah. Yetzirah is therefore an extremely busy place: it is where all the background work is done to ensure that a venture will succeed. If Atziluth is the fertilized embryo and Briah the womb, then Yetzirah is the channelled energy that is directed into the formation of the embryonic child.

Psychologists—following the lead of Sigmund Freud—have joined the conscious exploration of the Yetziratic realm. In many instances, what are new psychological insights have in fact been recognized for centuries in the Mysteries, but new exploration has made this world more accessible to more people. There have recently been some interesting speculations about the nature of the Internet and virtual reality: it has been suggested that these could give rise one day to a fully conscious Yetzirah.

The lower face of Yetzirah is the realm of the ego: we live most of our time in this area of the ladder—it is the region of the "inner life" and is therefore the most recognizable area of Yetzirah. The upper face of Yetzirah is beyond our direct experience for most of the time; beyond the Veil. It is the realm of the higher self or guardian angel.

Walking across the earth, we spend most of our lives experiencing the physical world of Assiah.

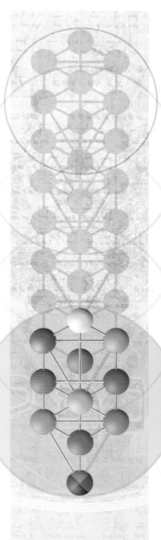

Assiah, World of Earth and Experience
The Planets

Assiah is where the journey of creation ends, and the journey of return starts. The world in Assiah represents the physical plane, and everything that happens there, from our physical body and our senses to nature, technology, art, society, war, and politics. All the actions of the physical plane are Assiatic in nature, although their causes will originate from the other worlds.

Assiah is the world of "making," where the archetypes, energies, patterns, and forces of the higher worlds have manifested in the stuff of this world. The element here is Earth, the least dynamic and most static of the four elements.

Water is associated with Yetzirah, the world of emotion. Sometimes calm, sometimes powerful, it is difficult to control and will take on any shape.

Most of us spend most of our time in Assiah. In the lower face, we are focused outward, toward the outer reality. The upper face is the lower face of Yetzirah, and this is the area of inner reflection.

The physical planets of our solar system correspond to the energies of the sephiroth in Assiah. When the ancients named the planets after their gods, they did not think the gods were literally up in the sky. Instead, they were convenient metaphors for powerful, universal energies. This has been known and understood by the Mystery schools for thousands of years: most if not all of the stories of the gods, in all cultures, are actually teaching stories, used to help people to understand their world.

The next five chapters take us, stage by stage, up the Ladder of Light, through the 32 stages of the *Sepher Yetzirah* from the lowest level up to the very highest.

CHAPTER 3

Assiah, World of Experience

Assiah is the world of practical experience. Each stage in this chapter can be related to a direct experience through the physical senses. The exercises are the foundations on which the understanding and practice of Kabbalah are built. The next five chapters follow the Path of Return up the ladder, retracing the Path of Creation of the Lightning Flash. Each world making up the ladder comprises an entire tree, from Malkuth up to Kether.

Moving up the ladder in any world, beyond Chesed we reach the Abyss. Beyond the Abyss lies Binah. But no path crosses the Abyss from Chesed to Binah. So how do we progress? In keeping with the teaching of transcendence—"problems that cannot be solved, are transcended"—the Abyss can be crossed only by transcending the current world and moving into the next one: consciousness leaves Chesed of the current world, falls "through the looking glass," and arrives in the Yesod of the next.

Each chapter ends with Chesed, and the supernal sephiroth of each world—Binah, Chockmah, and Kether—is included at the beginning of the chapter following.

Assiah is the most practical and down-to-earth of all the worlds. It is also the world into which all Kabbalistic experience is brought. Kabbalah places great emphasis on direct, tangible experience.

This chapter looks at the seven lowest stages (32 to 26) that build the lower face of the Assiatic Tree. Each is described under three headings: Ladder, describing the sephira it represents on the Ladder of Light; Tree, describing the path it represents on the Tree of Life; and Exercise, describing how to experience the stage.

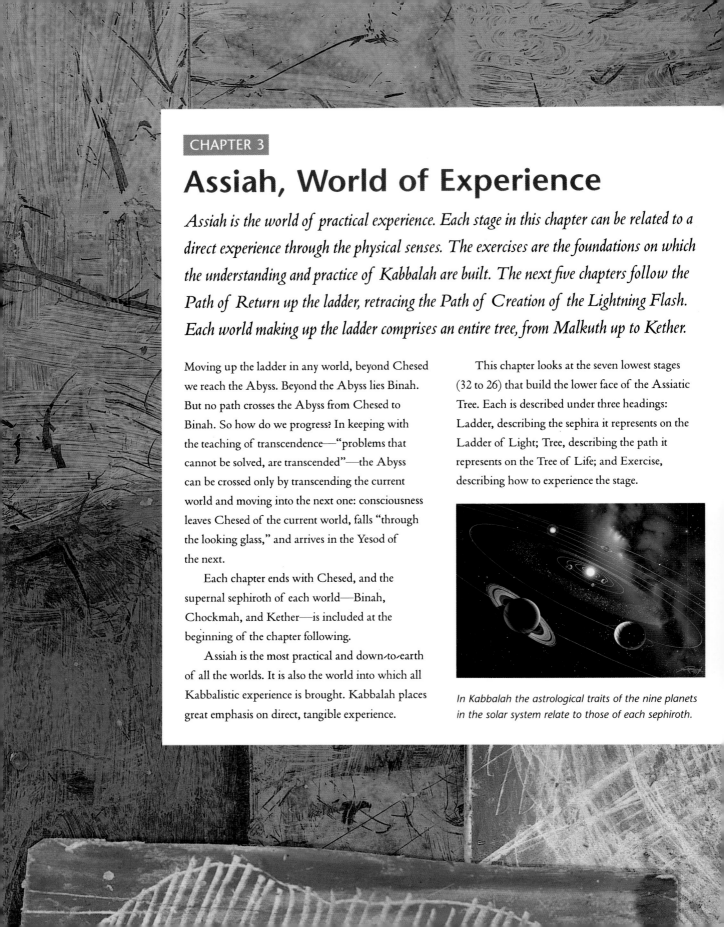

In Kabbalah the astrological traits of the nine planets in the solar system relate to those of each sephiroth.

Tarot and Astrology

The Tarot cards listed are the Major Arcana of the Tarot deck. These were originally attributed to the Paths by the French occultist Eliphas Levi . All Tarot descriptions used are taken from images of the Rider-Waite pack. This is the oldest and probably best-known of the modern tarot packs.

Although astrology is a spiritual teaching system in its own right, there are many parallels between it and Kabbalah, and the astrological qualities of the planets correspond to the qualities of each of the sephiroth. The ten sephiroth of Assiah, plus Da'ath, are each assigned one of the astrological planets.

The ancient astronomer/astrologers knew of only seven planets: these planets plus the Earth herself have ancient correspondences with the sephiroth, from Malkuth to Binah.

Since the 18th century, however, three new planets have been discovered (Uranus, Neptune, Pluto), as well as numerous asteroids and planetoids. Various Kabbalists have assigned these to the sephiroth, but there is no universal agreement as to the correct matches, so more than one is sometimes given (see pages 122–123 and table in the Correspondences section on pages 124–125).

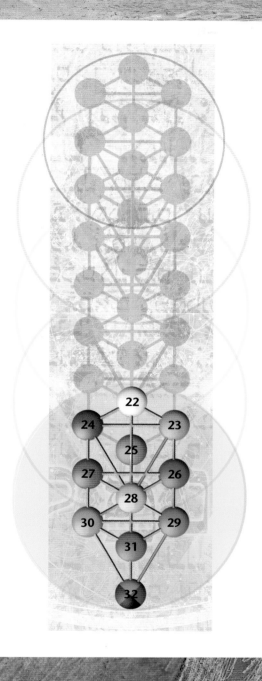

Our Path of Return up the Ladder of Light begins in Assiah, the world of experience, at the bottom of the Ladder.

Stage 32 The Experience of the Earth

"The beginning and the end." This is the last stage when moving down the ladder on the cycle of manifestation: in human terms this represents the physical body. But as the most material point anything can reach, it also represents the starting point of the return. Just as any journey starts with the first step, so this stage must be attended to on the journey up the ladder. In the body, this stage is the sense of touch. The lesson is, "Keep in touch."

Malkuth in Assiah, the first stage of our journey up the Ladder of Light.

The Earth: Malkuth in Assiah symbolizes this planet, which is at the very lowest point on the Ladder of Light, and also represents our physical body and the four elements.

Ladder *Malkuth in Assiah*

This is the very lowest point of the Ladder of Light, representing the densest form of God: this beautiful planet on which we live and move and have our being, and the entire cosmos of matter that surrounds us. It also represents our physical body and the four elements that flow through it—earth, water, air, and fire. These elements should not be confused with the chemical elements of modern science: they are represented on the tarot trump of this path: the World (sometimes called the Universe). This shows a woman surrounded by four animals. The figure is the Shekhinah, lost and far away from her lover.

Tree *Malkuth to Yesod*

This is a familiar journey that everybody makes, every day of his or her life: the journey from being awake to being asleep. We can take this journey in full consciousness, but that adventure belongs to the world of Yetzirah, and will be described there.

The first and most profound of all Kabbalistic teachings is that everything we need in order to

THE WORLD.

return to the Orchard is to be found right here and now. All we have to do is to live our life, fully and completely! This sounds straightforward, but in reality it is difficult. There are many distractions in life. Often we are so busy, we lose ourselves in ourselves, and forget the reality of life, which is very simple.

This reflects the virtue of Malkuth—discrimination: we need to be aware of the influences around us in order to discriminate between what is good and what is bad. (Of course, what usually happens is that it is too much effort, and so inertia, the vice of Malkuth, sets in.)

Hebrew Letter *Tau—Cross*

The cross is the cross of matter. Tau also has the meaning of a seal; something that makes an impression in a soft substance—such as a signet ring in sealing wax. This gives the sense of the earth, and of the world of Assiah itself, taking on the impression—the form—of the energies from the worlds above. In Christian Cabala, stage 32 is considered to represent the congregation in the church: the ordinary people.

EXERCISE BE HERE NOW

Before we can begin the journey back to the Orchard, we need to finish the journey of incarnation, and realize that we really are here on planet earth, in a physical body. We live too much in our heads, or our hearts, or someone else's head or heart—in fact, anywhere other than in our own body in our own life.

This exercise should be done gently—don't try too hard. In fact, don't "try" at all: we do not try to breathe, we just do it.

1. Decide in advance when, where, and for how long you will do the exercise. To begin, choose maybe 10 minutes at a time when you can be alone, with few distractions.
2. For the length of time you do the exercise, just be aware of what happens. If you are sitting, be aware that you are sitting. If you are walking or talking, just be aware of walking or talking.
3. Do not let anything that happens stop you from just doing the exercise, which is to be aware of what happens as you do what you are doing.
4. What did you notice? It will probably be this: we so easily lose ourselves. A thought enters our heads, or someone walks past, and suddenly we are living inside our head again, following the thought, or the person, and we have lost our self, out here in the real world. After a while of doing this, you may begin to notice that the "chattering monkey" of your mind occasionally slows down, giving you a glimpse of what it could be like to live in the moment.

Stage 31 The Experience of the Moon

The moon represents the experience of movement and flux. It is the fluid, rhythmic change to which all physical things are subject. In the body, this stage is the sense of smell and taste. The lesson of this stage is, "Go with the flow."

Ladder Yesod in Assiah

On the next step up the ladder, we start to move through time as well as space. Yesod, the sephira of the moon, introduces the cycles and patterns of change. It represents all the body systems that work without us needing to know about them, in a well-ordered, rhythmical way: from tissue growth to the heart's beat. It is also the level of the autonomic nervous system, from which comes the instinctive fight-or-flight mechanism.

In Yesod in Assiah, we experience movement and begin to understand the rhythm of change. Here we learn to "go with the flow."

The moon is ever-changing. Waxing and waning, sometimes illuminating and sometimes not, it teaches us to understand and accept change—so well do we learn this lesson that we often take it for granted.

Tree Malkuth to Hod

This path represents information received and passed on, that is to say, the process of communication. On a single tree the paths can work on multiple levels. Here, in the body this path represents the sensory organs (Malkuth) receiving stimuli and passing them through the nervous system, producing a reaction in thought (Hod).

In the psyche, this path could manifest by someone talking to a friend, and an idea forming in their mind. The mechanism is basically one of awakening.

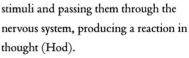 ### Hebrew Letter Shin— Flame/Tooth

This letter indicates the dancing, changing light around the dark coal or around the wick of a candle. The tooth is said to be representative of the power of both decay and entropy. These two images are considered to be symbols of the best and the worst of the experience that the moon provides, representing the experience of movement and flux.

EXERCISE BREATHING

There are many natural rhythms in our life: day and night, the moon's monthly cycles, the seasons of the year. Most of us live constantly in artificial light, air conditioning, and central heating. We lose awareness of natural rhythms and forget how important they are. The most immediate cycle, the one we take for granted, is the rhythm of breath.

Lives can be transformed by improving the rhythm of breathing. The change that can occur by tuning in to this—or any other—natural rhythm is well symbolized by the tarot trump Judgement. It shows an angel blowing a trumpet, flying over three figures emerging from the darkness, often out of the water, or from a coffin. It signifies awakening, a new beginning.

- How are you are breathing? Where is the movement? Most likely, you breathe by moving your rib cage in and out. Yet if you watch babies breathing, or watch someone sleeping, you will notice that it is their stomachs, not their chests, that rise and fall. This movement of the stomach is called diaphragmatic breathing: the diaphragm is a muscle that lies between the lungs and the stomach. When we are anxious, a lot of tension is held in the diaphragm, making it seize up and impossible to use for breathing. As a consequence, the breath becomes shallow and quick, and the body tenses up even more: it becomes a vicious circle.
- As you do the Be Here Now exercise on page 43, be aware of your breathing. Breathe from your diaphragm. It may feel unnatural and uncomfortable at first, but persevere: it will help to make your breathing slower and deeper, which will help you relax.
- Whenever you become aware of your breathing, during the day, at work, remember to change into diaphragmatic breathing. Try to Be Here Now as well! You may find that, as the breathing relaxes you, your Be Here Now exercise gets easier, and the "chattering monkey" of your mind starts to still itself at times.

Stage 30 The Experience of Mercury

Astrologically, Mercury represents the mind, connecting and interpreting experience. In the physical body, the experience of this stage is the sense of sight. Reading, insight, communications, and technology are all related to this stage of the ladder.

Ladder *Hod in Assiah*

On the next step on the journey back to the Orchard, we reach Hod in Assiah. This represents the process of communication in the physical body: nerves, which send electrical signals; and hormones, the chemical messengers in the bloodstream.

Hod is the realm of Mercury. The planet Mercury is the innermost planet of our solar system; it is small and moves very fast, very close to the sun. In Greek mythology, Hermes, his counterpart, had a very close relationship with Apollo, the Sun God. Hermes was also the messenger of the gods, traveling between Olympus, Heaven, and Earth, and able to enter Hades, the Underworld.

Tree *Yesod to Hod*

Here is the start of the orange Hermetic teaching ray, moving through Hod and down to Yesod. This path demands self-knowledge of all its disciples. "Man— Know Thyself" was written above the door of all Temples of the Hermetic mysteries. The tarot card assigned to this path is the Sun, indicating that we receive the first illumination from our true self through self-examination.

What good is it waking up in the middle of the night with an extraordinary insight that will save the world, only to go back to sleep and the following morning discover that you have forgotten what it was? It is the combination of intelligence and memory—Hod and Yesod—that gives us the ability to learn.

We take reading and writing for granted these days. Yet only a few generations ago, they were considered quite extraordinary skills that took very special training and enormous dedication to acquire. The act of reading and writing short-circuits the old ways of learning by rote or memory (so much so that it is unusual if someone can remember all the words to a favorite poem, or song, these days).

A Kabbalistic term for writing is "Black Fire on White Fire," recognizing the fact that the written word can transform lives just as profoundly as a physical fire can transform matter. On many spiritual paths, it is very important to keep a written note of your experiences.

Hebrew Letter *Resh— Head/Beginning*

The letter represents the workings of thought in the brain. The Resh is also thought of as a "bent-over" head, indicating the work involved in converting insights and intuitions into speech and the written word.

In Hod in Assiah, we interpret our experience and learn to communicate. This is related to the sense of sight.

Mercury is the closest planet to the sun and completes a full orbit in just 88 days.

THE SUN

KEEPING A JOURNAL

Some simple guidelines for keeping a journal, or spiritual diary, are as follows:

- Keep your journal close by you when you are meditating, and by your bed at night: dreams can bring very significant messages and teachings.
- Write notes in your journal as close to the time of the experience as is possible.
- The most boring dream, the most difficult meditation, can turn out to be the most important of your life, so do not think, "I will not bother writing that one down." You may not understand it now, but it may help you profoundly later on.
- Treat your journal with respect: use it only for special things such as recording dreams or insights from meditations and spiritual exercises. Do not use it to write out a shopping list, or pull a sheet out to mop up a spilled drink.
- Keeping a journal is part of the process, not separate from it. Insights and understandings that come as you are writing are just as important as the experience you are writing about, so make a note of them as well.

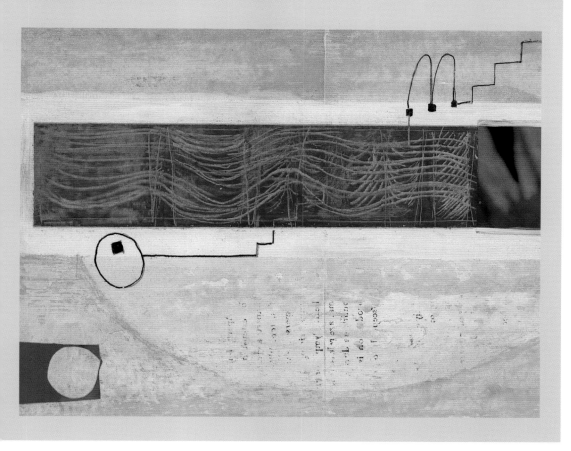

Stage 29 The Experience of Venus

In the body, this stage is represented by the sense of hearing. Sounds can sometimes evoke strong passions: this experience is most strongly associated with the planet Venus. This stage is intimately connected with creation: so on one level it is to do with sexual expression, but more generally, it is anything to do with bringing those creative urges into manifestation.

Netzach in Assiah is associated with passion that leads to creativity.

Ladder *Netzach in Assiah*

The planet Venus is probably the most beautiful nighttime sight—by far the brightest star in the sky because she sets shortly after or rises shortly before the Sun. The goddess Venus—or Aphrodite (her Greek name)—is the goddess of Love: astrologically, she rules the realm of the emotions, including love and passion. At the level of Assiah, it is passion rather than love that is the strongest influence.

Netzach in Assiah represents the processes of movement in the physical body. It is your limbs moving your body around the world. The level of consciousness is that of an animal in the jungle, ready to eat, watching out for predators: this is nature, red in tooth and claw.

Tree *Malkuth to Netzach*

The nature of this path is well expressed by the tarot card associated with it: the Moon. This shows a dog and a wolf together, both of whom are howling at a large full moon. The domesticated dog is at home by the warm fire of Malkuth; the wolf expresses the full-flowing "life on the wild side" energy of Netzach. They meet to howl together on this path.

Venus is visible as a bright morning or evening star from the earth. Its extremely hot surface is shrouded in dark cloud that adds to its beauty.

Hebrew Letter *Qoph, the Back of the head*

At the back of the head lies the most primitive part of the brain, the hind-brain. This is the source of our most deeply felt urges and instinctive reactions: it is at the back of the head and neck that the "hackles rise" on hearing a particularly evocative sound—such as the baying of a wolf.

EXERCISE STRETCH/RELAX

Creation can be on many different levels. Whenever I sit down to do any writing, I find it a lot easier if there is no mess of papers on or around my desk. Clutter is distracting and working around it wastes energy. So it is with the tensions that we carry around in the muscles of our body, especially in the shoulders, or the neck: they are the body equivalent of desk clutter! This exercise is based on the principle that we feel better after we have dealt with the clutter. Do this exercise any time you are feeling stressed—physically, emotionally, or mentally.

1. Sit or lie quietly and comfortably for a while; do the Be Here Now exercise until you feel calm and relaxed.
2. Think about your toes. Tense them up as hard as you can, while keeping the rest of your body as relaxed as you can. Hold the tension for at least one long in-breath.
3. As you breathe out, release your toes, relaxing the muscles completely.
4. Now do the same for your ankle and calf muscles: tense them up as hard as you possibly can on the in-breath, then relax them on the out-breath.
5. Do this for every group of muscles in your body, working up from the feet, through the thighs, buttocks, genitals, stomach, lower back, rib cage; hands, lower arms, upper arms; upper back and shoulders, neck, jaw, cheeks and nose, eyes, forehead, and scalp.
6. If any group of muscles feel like they are not relaxed, repeat the exercise a couple of times before moving on to the next group.

Stage 28 The Experience of the Sun

The central point of the world of Assiah is found at this stage. At the core of any experience lies the seed of the next step: here at the center of material experience can be found the start of the next level, the ground of consciousness. In the body, this stage is the sense of balance.

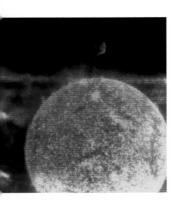

At the center of the tree of Assiah, Stage 28 is also the base of the tree of Yetzirah.

Ladder *Tiphareth in Assiah, Malkuth in Yetzirah*

As the sun is the center of the solar system, so Tiphareth (balance) in Assiah sits at the center of the material world. Physically, this point represents the solar plexus, at the center of the body; the heart, the center of the circulatory system; and the central nervous system.

Just as there can be no life on earth once the sun has died, once the heart has stopped beating and the brain and brain stem have died, there is no life left in the body.

The brain can be considered as the physical expression of our psychological existence: it is fitting therefore that this stage also includes Malkuth (body) in Yetzirah (the psychological world).

Tree *Yesod to Netzach*

On this path we find the start of the green, Orphic teaching ray, moving between Netzach (passion) and Yesod (feeling). This path has a very different quality to that of the Hermetic Mysteries—it is the path of the artist rather than the scholar.

The Rites of Orpheus were inspirational affairs, with a heavy emphasis on self-expression and creativity: Orpheus was the lyre player of the gods who went down to Hades—the Greek world of the dead—in search of his wife, Eurydice.

In one way or another, all artists need to descend into Hades to discover their muse. This is what the tarot card the Star is about: the guiding light, far above us that guides us—if we can remember to look.

The Star woman on this tarot card is shown pouring water from two large vessels into the earth and this activity can be considered to represent bringing life and inspiration to the recipient.

THE STAR.

Hebrew Letter *Tzaddi—the Hunt, the Fish Hook*

The name of this letter alludes to the search of Orpheus and the quality of the green ray that starts at this stage: the artist has to hunt down his muse. She will not be found on a printed page, but must be angled for, patiently and without knowing when the divine inspiration will come.

The Sun, around which the planets in our system revolve.

EXERCISE THE GARDEN OF CONSCIOUSNESS

When we are balanced and at peace in our bodies (Tiphareth in Assiah), we are ready to explore the inner kingdom (Malkuth in Yetzirah). The Garden of Consciousness exercise is common to many teachings. It introduces a safe place, located inside ourselves, where we can go to receive inner healing, advice, insight, and other blessings. The following steps describe how to get there:

1 Find yourself a place where you can sit in comfort and peace, for between 15 and 30 minutes, without any disturbances. Have your journal with you.

2 Start with the Stretch/Relax or any other relaxation exercise.

3 Use your Breathing and Be Here Now exercises, or any other technique you may know, to make yourself feel peaceful and relaxed.

4 Imagine yourself in a garden. It is more likely to be somewhere you have not consciously known before, although it might be a garden in a place that you have visited physically. This is your inner garden.

5 Explore your inner garden. Do plants and flowers grow there? Which ones? What size is the garden? What are the boundaries like? Does it have a high wall? Rolling fields beyond? Nothing? This is your garden: everything is allowed.

6 All ways of experiencing your garden are valid. You may see the grass, listen to the wind or the birds, smell the flowers, feel the ground beneath your feet, or hear a voice describing your garden. Try to include as many of these inner senses as you can, to build up as strong an impression of your garden as you can.

Simply reading through this exercise will give a flavor of it. On some level, you were doing it as you read. The images/experience of it are already working in you, to create a place of peace, at the very center of your being.

Stage 27 The Experience of Mars

This stage represents the qualities of concentration, focus, and action. Mars is known as the "red planet," because it glows with a dull-red color. Mars was the Roman god of War, red being the color of blood. Not surprisingly then, in the body, the energy of Mars is in the blood, and provides us with the energy to work our muscles. On a physical level, it is the positional sense of knowing where the limbs are.

At Geburah in Assiah we concentrate and find the energy for action.

Ladder *Geburah in Assiah*

It may seem puzzling that Geburah (severity) is on the pillar of form, not of force (see pages 30–31), but this is correct. An animal fights only when cornered: it would far rather use its Geburah to run away. The martial arts, oriented toward self-defense, are a far clearer expression of this stage: aggression and violence are a misuse of Geburah/Martian energy.

The surface of Mars, the Red Planet, is marked with dark red patches and two white polar caps. The red is associated with blood in the body.

Tree *Hod to Netzach*

This path is the first to link sephiroth on opposite sides of the tree. It is therefore a path of high energy, to do with balancing the masculine and feminine energies. The tarot trump here is the Tower, which shows what can happen if the energies are not in balance.

The card shows two people falling from a high tower which is being struck by lightning. This stage is the balancing act between Netzach (passion) and Hod (thought). Too much Netzach in our lives can bring chaos. Too much Hod can bring dry routine and a narrowed vision. We need to focus on what is needed in our lives to keep the balance just right.

Hebrew Letter
Peh—The Mouth

This letter looks like a mouth, with a little tongue inside. The mouth, and the voice that comes from it, can be an active expression of our thoughts and feelings, helping to find the right balance.

EXERCISE OPENINGS, CLOSINGS AND CONCENTRATION

The exercises in this chapter can take us into a different state of mind from the everyday consciousness. It is important to keep this time of meditation and the time of living separate to avoid feeling disoriented. Using words and/or gestures that signal the opening and closing of a meditation do help the transition. An excellent gesture is the sign of the Cross. If you do not wish to use this, use something of your own or the Kabbalistic cross, which is described below.

- Close your eyes and pause for a while. Put your hands together, fingers up at your chest.
- Raise your right hand to your forehead, touch it and say, "Ateh" ("to you").
- Lower your hand to your solar plexus, touch it and say, "Malkuth" ("the Kingdom").
- Move your hand to your right shoulder, touch it and say, "ve Geburah" ("and Power").
- Move your hand to your left shoulder, touch it and say, "ve Gedulah" ("and Glory").
- Make a small circle in the air in front of you, and say, "le Olahim" ("in eternity").
- Join your hands together and say, "Amen." Open your eyes and pause for a while.

The following is an exercise of concentration.
- Find a place where you can sit, for about 15 minutes, in comfort and peace.
- Move into your inner world by using your chosen opening gesture, and words.
- Choose any short, simple phrase, no more than five words, and say it to yourself. Repeat over and over, concentrating on the words.
- Every time that you find yourself thinking about something else, come back to your phrase.
- When the time is up, use your own closing gesture and words, open your eyes, and bring yourself back to the outside world.

Concentrating on the phrase is more difficult than it sounds, but it is very good practice for doing other exercises higher up the ladder.

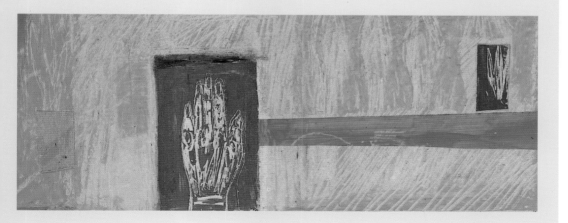

Stage 26 The Experience of Jupiter

In Roman mythology, Jupiter is the father of the gods, and watches with a benevolent eye over all of humankind. This stage brings a very positive energy, with enormous benefits—but there can be a down side too. This is the highest level to be reached entirely within the material world of Assiah: it can seem that there is nowhere else to go, nothing more to be learned. If people believe this in the good times, it can become a trap when the luck runs out.

Chesed in Assiah marks the highest stage on the ladder that is entirely within Assiah.

Jupiter, the largest of the planets, moves in a slow orbit around the sun.

Ladder *Chesed in Assiah*

This sephira has been called the Lord of the Gates of Matter. Chesed is the first sephira wholly in the world of Assiah and no other on the way down the ladder, and is therefore the last wholly in Assiah on the way back up. Here is the place of the first real test for individuals on a spiritual quest.

Tree *Hod to Tiphareth*

This path takes us—for the first time—out of the world of normal, everyday experience, to something beyond. Occultists call the experience of this and the next two paths the "dark night of the soul." On this path we begin to experience energies that are definitely beyond normal consciousness.

When a person takes a decision to walk the path of Return, they will start to experience everyday things on another level. For example, they might start to realize that some of the forces "out there," which "do things to us" are actually something else.

Take the idea of the Devil. The tarot trump of that name, which is associated with this stage, shows a man and a woman chained to a great devil form. Stage 26 is partly to do with the common illusion that material possessions can make us happy. The devil in the card is a devil of our own making: the chains are ours to keep or to cast off. The things of this earth cannot make us happy: if we try to find happiness through possessions, we will end up being enslaved by them, or at least by our desire for them.

Once we are in control of this inner devil, rather than him being in control of us, he will bring us great benefit.

Astrologically, Jupiter is called the "Great Benefic," and his influence is extremely positive. For Jupiter's benefits to flow, we have to be generous—both with ourselves and with our possessions.

Hebrew Letter
Ayin—the Eye

This letter is considered to represent the eye of God, who is thought to be looking down on the material world, and seeing "that it is good."

EXERCISE LETTING GO

We all have material things—great and small—that we are "attached" to, for all sorts of reasons. Think about these things for a moment. Then consider, for each one:

- Why do you hang on to it?
- How would you cope if it were taken away?
- Can you think of any situation in which you would give it away?
- How hard is it for you to let this object out of your life?

A young man was looking for a Maggid, a teacher of Kabbalah. He went to visit a Maggid who had an excellent reputation. When he got there, the house was enormous, and the teacher came to see him wearing expensive robes and jewelry. The student felt uncomfortable with this, made his excuses and left.

After a while, he found a poor Maggid to study under, and he told him about the rich man he had met. "Ah yes," said the poor Maggid, "I know of him: he is very great indeed. He has evolved to a stage where the things of this world do not matter to him. Whereas I, who still have attachments to worldly things, must stay poor in order to keep on the path."

This stage marks the end of the first part of the journey, through the material world of Assiah. Within the tree of this world, there is no clear path to the next sephiroth, Binah, which is beyond the Abyss. In order to progress, it is necessary to move into the next world, the psychological realm of Yetzirah.

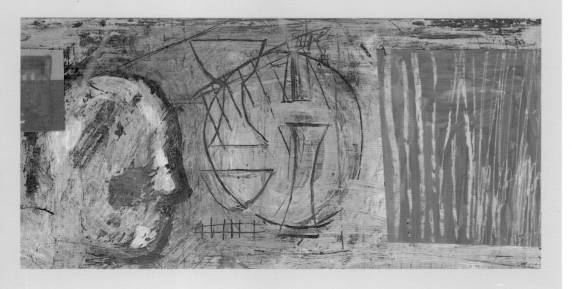

CHAPTER 4

Yetzirah, World of Consciousness

The realm of Yetzirah is the realm of feelings and imagery. It sits between creation (Briah) and form (Assiah). The beings traditionally associated with Yetzirah are the angels. Their function is to take the ideas of Briah and to act upon them, the results of these actions finally appearing in Assiah.

The good and evil angels, struggling for the possession of a child, by William Blake (1757–1827).

This chapter looks at the seven stages of Yetzirah—25 to 20—that together build the lower face of the Yetziratic tree. As in the Assiah chapter, each section covers one stage, under the headings: Ladder, describing the sephira it represents on the Ladder of Light; Tree, describing the path it represents on the Tree of Life; and Visualization, suggesting inner work to experience this stage.

Angels

Each sephira has a different rank of angels. We all have a certain picture of angels and often associate them with wings and harps—these are not the type of angels referred to here.

The German mystic and clairvoyant Rudolf Steiner (1861–1925) wrote about angels. He was not a Kabbalist, but the Kabbalah was one of the traditions he drew on. To him, angels were part of the evolution of the universe: the ranks of angels stretched right up to beings that could directly perceive God, in Kether. In Steiner's cosmology, the tenth and lowest rank of angel deals with physical reality. That rank is us: humanity. In Kabbalah, the same idea applies: the rank of angelic beings of the Malkuth of Yetzirah are the Ashim (the souls of fire). These are individuals who have reached the stage where they do not need a body, yet wish to continue to work with the evolution of this planet on as close to a physical level as possible. Each angelic order is ranked up the sephiroth (see pp. 124–125).

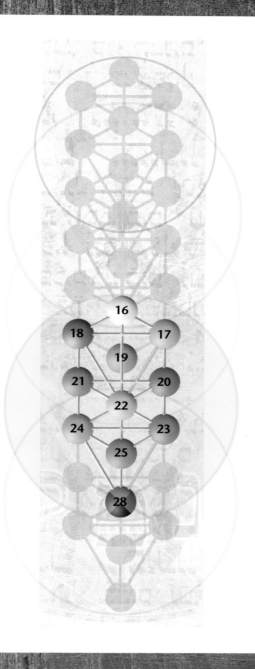

Stage 25 The Consciousness of the Kerubim

This stage is the start of the realm of the psyche. At this level of consciousness there is the opportunity to view the ego objectively, relative to the rest of the self. The name "Kerubim" translates as "The Strong": these angels act as the "Foundation" stones of our psyche, aiding illumination and understanding of this stage.

At the cross-over point between Assiah and Yetzirah, Stage 25 is where the ego and self meet.

Ladder *Yesod in Yetzirah, Da'ath in Assiah*

At Da'ath in Assiah, we have knowledge of the body and the material world. It is a common mistake to confuse knowledge with wisdom and understanding: ego-consciousness often feels that it knows everything that there is to know about everything. Yesod in Yetzirah is the ground from which the ego grows.

Tree *Yesod to Tiphareth*

The light of the self shines down this path onto the ego in Yesod (feeling). If we can open ourselves to this place, much healing can come to us. The tarot card associated with this stage is Temperance. It shows an angel pouring water from one container into another, and is to do with balancing the energies that meet here—Assiah and Yetzirah on the ladder, and Yesod and Tiphareth (balance) either side of the veil on the single tree.

Once there was a coachman who looked after his master's coach and horse extremely well. The master went away on a long journey, and in time the coachman forgot who owned the coach and horse, or even who paid him. He imagined himself to be the master, and dressed up in finery and went around pretending—but felt everybody could tell he was just a coachman. He felt ashamed and put on even finer clothes, and even more airs and graces. Finally, the master returned, and wanted to be taken out in his coach and horse. But the coachman was out drinking. He had forgotten to feed the horse, and had left the coach out and let it rust.

The ego is an excellent coachman, under the good and constant influence of the self. Without that guidance, it can become a very bad master. This becomes most apparent in times of stress.

Simple, honest folk with a strong religious belief or moral code, with no pretensions of being something they are not, usually fare better in extremely stressful situations than those people who build their lifestyles on social niceties and false identities.

Hebrew Letter

Samech, the Prop

This letter is traditionally linked to the vision of the Patriarch Jacob, who fell asleep and saw a vision of a ladder reaching from the Earth right up to Heaven, with angels traveling up and down upon it. Samech represents the aid we can be given in reaching farther, deeper, higher into ourselves. After all, a ladder is nothing more than a series of props.

TEMPERANCE.

VISUALIZATION CHANGING MOODS

If you are not used to checking, it is not always easy to know how your inner psyche is feeling. Until you get used to being in regular—conscious—contact with these parts of yourselves, the following exercise will help.

1. Find a place where you can sit for between 15 and 30 minutes in comfort and peace, without any disturbances. Have your journal with you.

2. After any preliminary preparation of relaxation and centering, perform your opening (see page 53) and find yourself in your Garden of Consciousness.

3. Find a place in your garden where you can sit and feel at peace.

4. This time, pay particular attention to the environment. What time of day is it? What is the weather like? How do you feel, being in your garden, right now?

5. When you have finished, close your meditation (see page 53). Note down your experience in your journal.

This exercise should be repeated for at least a week. See if you can notice any link between how the garden feels, and your worldly experience. Did you have an argument the day your garden was covered in thunderclouds? Was the garden beautiful and sunny when friends came to visit and you had a lovely time? Note any correlations—or any mismatches—in your journal.

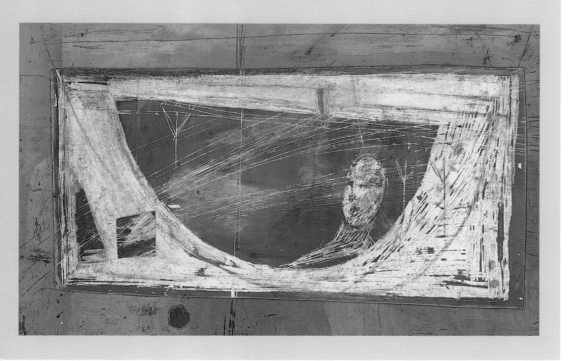

Stage 24 The Consciousness of the Beni-Elohim

This stage, which is also associated with the ego, represents the workings of the mind. Thoughts can be used both to liberate the soul and to bind it. At this stage, both types of thoughts are explored. The Beni-Elohim are the Sons of God; the same angels who were said to have mated with the "Daughters of Man" in the Old Testament. These beings aid our thoughts, and guide us rather as wise elders would.

This is the stage where thoughts are formed and then organized.

Ladder *Hod in Yetzirah, Binah in Assiah*

An enormous number of pathways between brain cells are destroyed during the first three years of life, the time of early socialization and learning of language. As particular pathways are used more and more often, concrete thought processes (Hod in Yetzirah) can start. The organizational function (Binah in Assiah) then severs the less well-used, distracting links between the cells, so that thought flow can become more efficient.

Of course, this efficiency increase comes at a price. One example is the sounds that are common in some languages but unknown in others: if a child does not grow up hearing these sounds, it will be difficult to reproduce them when learning languages later in life—the pathways in the brain will not exist. This is why people who learn languages when they are older speak with accents: they are using the pathways developed for their own language.

Tree *Netzach to Tiphareth*

This path represents the journey from ego-consciousness to self-consciousness. Netzach is to do with the will (often channeled in selfish ways) to get what the ego wants. This path reiterates the lesson of stage 25, that the ego is a servant of the self.

There are strong associations with death on this path, for the ego is terrified that if it loses control, it risks its own destruction. Hence the connection with the tarot card Death, the Grim Reaper.

The experiences of childhood deeply affect the adult that a child becomes, but are buried in the recesses of the psyche. Yet for most people the child they were is dead—part of a life that is no more.

The inner child is a universal image, which can hold those parts of the individual that have not yet been expressed. It is therefore a repository of hope and ideals—and an inspiration for what a person can become in the future. We have within us everything that we need on the journey of Return. Qualities that have been buried by the Ego are still available to us through the inner child: all we have to do is ask.

Hebrew Letter
Nun, the Fish

The fish lives in a realm in which humans cannot survive: it is cold although living things are supposed to be warm. To the ancients therefore the fish was a symbol of the underworld and the afterlife.

VISUALIZATION THE INNER CHILD

This meditation makes use of the Garden of Consciousness to explore the inner you. It will take up to 20 minutes.

1. After relaxing and centering, think briefly about how life was for you up to the age of five. Bring to mind how things were for you then. Open your meditation, and find yourself back in your Garden of Consciousness. Go and sit in your "at home" place.

2. Now call out to your inner child and invite it to come to you in your garden. Wait quietly for a figure to appear.

3. Does your inner child look how you expected? Speak to the child: is he or she shy, excited, sad?

4. If anything seems to be troubling your inner child, ask if you can help. With an adult's perspective, you may be able to help.

5. When you have finished talking with your inner child, say thank you, and ask the figure to leave your garden. Finish by closing the meditation (see page 53).

This meditation may be repeated as often as is useful to you. It may be that the first time you try, no images or sense of your inner child comes to you. If this is the case, do not give up; try again the next day. Pay particular attention to your dreams: the inner child may come to you there if he or she does not come to the Garden.

Stage 23 The Consciousness of the Elohim

The 23rd stage has two sides. One brings creativity and self-expression; the other demands attention and awareness. The power of either can turn our everyday world topsy-turvy. The order of angels of this stage are the Elohim, meaning "Gods." Their work can be experienced in our dreams, and in our imagination, as they create the images that we see and hear with our inner eyes and ears.

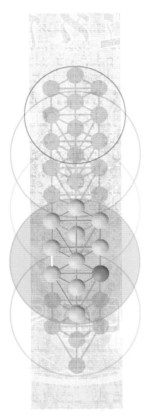

At this stage, appreciation of the emotions is uppermost and thought stimulates us to express ourselves.

Ladder *Netzach in Yetzirah, Chockmah in Assiah*

Until very recently, scientific wisdom held that we begin life with a fixed number of brain cells at birth, and that these cells die off throughout our lives and are not replaced.

A recent study has shown that our brains do grow new cells. Several things affect the level of growth: depression and forced learning slows it down, stimulation and voluntary learning is believed to enhance it.

This shows beautifully the action of Netzach (passion) in Yetzirah (the psychological world). If we are interested and excited about something, the energy flows and it becomes easy. This in turn stimulates Chockmah (wisdom) in Assiah (the physical world): the principle of organic life, the creative burst that urges the cells in our bodies to grow and multiply.

Tree *Hod to Geburah*

This is a path of testing: the thoughts of Hod are being tested in the fire of Geburah (severity). A good analogy would be firing clay pots in a kiln: those pots that have been badly made, or made with poorly prepared clay, will shatter in the heat. On the

THE HANGED MAN.

other hand, those that survive will be strong and stable. The type of thought that has gone through this process is, at one extreme, the rigorous logic that is required for a mathematical proof. A more mundane example would be the checking of a map before setting out on a long and complicated journey for the first time.

When we walk this path with thoughts not up to the required standard, the experience is symbolized by the tarot trump the Hanged Man: everything in our world can turn upside down. It demands we take a new view on life: the old one will not survive. The Hanged Man also represents a change within the person's consciousness from outward conquest to inward acceptance.

Hebrew Letter *Mem, Water*

This letter also means "fountain of Wisdom." It is one of the three mother letters from which all creation springs. Without water there is no life. Creativity is the key.

VISUALIZATION WORKING IN THE GARDEN

In previous meditations, we have simply experienced the Garden. Now we are ready to do some work in it, to make it even more beautiful and vibrant.

1. After relaxing and centering, perform your opening (see page 53) and find yourself back in your Garden of Consciousness. Have your journal with you.

2. This time, instead of going to your "at home" place, walk around your garden, and look at the growing things there. Ask yourself if anything could be improved in your garden.

3. If there are flowers, smell their scent. Give the trees a hug and feel their strength. Stroke animals, and play with them or, if they will not approach you, be understanding. They may still have to get used to you.

4. You may not have enough plants or animals. Or you may have too many, or some that do not seem to fit? Plant seeds, and find out what they have grown into the next time you visit, or call up an image of what you would like—just as you did with your inner child. And you can remove things. You are the gardener, the keeper of this place: you can decide what is here, and what is not.

5. When you have finished, close your meditation (see page 53) and return your attention to the outside world.

As you record what you have experienced in your garden, be mindful of what each plant or animal might mean to you in your life. Everything is in your Garden for a reason, and it was all created by you, even though you were not aware of it at the time.

Stage 22 The Consciousness of the Malachim

The first great meeting point of worlds on the ladder, this stage is at the center of the psyche. It defines the essence of the physical body, and gives the first glimmerings of the true self. The consciousness of this stage is one of bringing together, and healing—making whole. The name "Malachim," the order of Angels of Tiphareth in Yetzirah, translates as "Kings." The meaning here is focus of energy: these beings let consciousness be directed, and hold the sense of wholeness, of how things ought to be, of how they naturally relate to each other.

At this stage, three worlds meet—those of experience, consciousness, and mind.

Ladder *Tiphareth in Yetzirah, Kether in Assiah, Malkuth in Briah*

This is the first stage at which three worlds meet. Here we have the kingdom (Malkuth) of the mind, the center (Tiphareth) of the psyche and the crown (Kether) of the body.

Tree *Tiphareth to Geburah*

The key to this stage is simple: consciousness. It is about awareness of who we are, and what we are about. Once we have this level of awareness, our experience is represented by the tarot trump of this stage: Justice. The figure of Justice, carrying the sword and scales, is usually shown blindfolded, signifying impartiality: the law makes no distinction between people on account of who they are. Another interpretation of this symbol, however, is that a blindfolded person represents someone with everyday consciousness: they are blind to the higher realities. The figure in the tarot card therefore has their eyes open, representing the higher, truer justice that can only be found on an inner level.

At this stage we start to move through the veil between the self and the ego. According to the Bible, when Adam and Eve ate of the Tree of Knowledge, they were cast out of the Garden, and God made animal skins for them to wear. This is the fall of humankind down into Assiah—the world of flesh. The ego is the Yetziratic (psychological) tool we need to use in order to function in Assiah (the material world), but Briah (the mental world) is our natural place.

The experience of this stage is the realization that we are not only our body, or feelings, or thoughts. We can start to get a sense of the essence of ourselves: the inner spark within our beings that can never die.

Hebrew Letter
Lamed, the Ox-goad

This letter has two independent but complementary meanings. On the one hand, an ox-goad keeps the ox on the path, on the other, it can have a carrot dangling from the end. Lamed represents both the firm hand giving direction, and the aspiration of those people who seek the truth.

VISUALIZATION HEALING

Invite symbols of your body, feelings, and thoughts into your Garden of Consciousness to discover their separateness. Visualizing them as a form enables you to heal and be healed by them.

1. After relaxing and centering, find yourself back in your Garden of Consciousness, and go and sit in your "at home" place. Have your journal with you.
2. With your imagination, call out for an image which represents your body. Welcome the image into the Garden. It may look just like you, or it may be a completely abstract figure.
3. Use as many senses as you can. Notice what the figure looks like and listen to what it says.
4. Ask the figure what you can do to help it work better in you life. Again, use all of your senses to find the reply: the figure may not speak, but could give an answer through a movement or a scent.
5. Ask for a gift of healing: something that represents the gifts that your body gives to you in your daily life.
6. The figure may need healing. If it does, place your hands on the figure, and visualize a white light shining out of your fingers, surrounding it with warmth and comfort.
7. When you have finished communicating with the form, thank it, and ask it to leave.
8. Repeat this exercise with a figure that represents your feelings.
9. Repeat this exercise with a figure that represents your thoughts.

This meditation can be repeated as many times as you wish. The images that appear might be the same ones every time, or they may change—you will get used to the rules of your own inner world, and know what to expect in time.

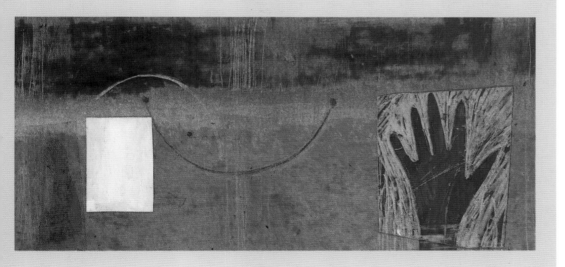

Stage 21 The Consciousness of the Seraphim

This stage represents the testing of the psyche on the anvil of experience. Below this level of the ladder, each individual is a separate entity. From here up, individuals start to interact with each other to a greater and greater extent. The angels of this stage are the Seraphim: the name translates as "Fiery Serpents."

At Stage 21 our ability to control our reactions is tested by experience, which is sometimes painful but always helpful.

Ladder *Geburah in Yetzirah*

Geburah in the realm of the psyche indicates our ability to control our reactions. A well-integrated, consciously functioning Geburah will show in a skillful debater, for example, always conscious of the opponent's arguments, judging both when to speak out and when to hold back. After Adam and Eve had been thrown out of Paradise, tradition states that it was the Seraphim who guarded the gates with fiery swords, so that they could not return.

In order to make the journey back to the Orchard, these swords of the Seraphim have to be faced: we have to accept the possibility that anything to which we are still attached will be burned away. These beings work on the distinctions between different aspects of ourselves, separating those aspects of personality that are necessary from those that are not. This process happens constantly in our lives, through external events; situations that seem to be guided from "outside." When we begin the path of return consciously, through this stage we begin to realize that all the hurt and pain we experience is created by our own angels, for our greater good.

Tree *Netzach to Chesed*

On this path we discover our sense of adventure. Netzach, the sephira of energy and life, moves toward Chesed, the sephira of expansion. This is the optimism of youth, about to be tested on the road of experience, and anything might happen: success, failure—it is all a possibility. Hence the attribution of the Wheel of Fortune tarot trump to this path.

At some point on the path of return, we need to move on from the realm that we know. In order to move on, we need to face risk, to take a gamble. We need to go on a quest.

This quality is well represented in the tales of King Arthur and the Knights of the Round Table. The Knights would take on quests to save a damsel, fight a dragon or an evil Knight, or right a wrong in the world.

Hebrew Letter
Kaph, the Palm of the Hand

The power of the hand is in its adaptability: it is used to wield many different instruments that can either create or destroy. Another translation of this letter is "Crown"—both translations together give the image of a hand over a head, in the act of giving a blessing—or a curse.

VISUALIZATION THE INNER QUEST

This meditation takes us for the first time out of the garden to the world beyond. This realm is just as much "us" as the garden, but is beyond those parts of ourselves with which we are immediately familiar. The visualization is timed, so as well as having your journal with you, have an alarm clock by your side.

1 Set your clock for 20 minutes.

2 After relaxing and centering, take yourself to your Garden of Consciousness, and go and sit in your "at home" place.

3 You may have noticed, at the boundaries of your garden, an opening to the world beyond. If you have not noticed it before, look, for it is there now. Beyond the opening you can see a path, leading up into the hills beyond.

4 In your mind's eye, imagine what it would be like to walk this path. What adventures, what excitement might there be while taking this journey? Where might the path lead?

5 Walk out along this path, knowing that you walk with the fiery sword of the Seraphim at your side. Greet any figures you meet in the same way that you greeted the images in the previous stage (22).

6 When the alarm goes, make your way back to your garden and then bring yourself back to everyday consciousness.

Following this path can take you on many extraordinary adventures. Remember to record in your journal everything that happens to you.

Stage 20 The Consciousness of the Chasmalim

Stage 20 puts an individual's experience in the context of others. Through social interaction—whether through the teacher/pupil relationship or among peers—people can achieve more than by working on their own. At this stage it is important not only to learn from others, but to have a good teacher—if we can communicate well with our teacher, we will eventually become properly equipped to hand our knowledge on to our friends and colleagues.

At this stage, we learn how our experiences relate to those of other people and are reminded that we do not act alone.

Ladder Chesed in Yetzirah

The Chasmalim—the "Bright Shining Ones"—work on the bonds between people and within groups. Their brightness of these angels is the brightness of that warmth felt between good friends or well-acquainted colleagues. The gift of this stage is to perfect oneself in a skill or profession. We are still on the quest, initiated at stage 21, but now we are well on the road. The scientist and the artist benefit equally here from the expansion that takes place in us.

The most important thing to have as we develop a particular skill is a good teacher: this stage enhances the communication between teacher and pupil. As we grow and learn and become more skillful, we can in turn pass our knowledge and powers of creation to others.

Tree Tiphareth to Chesed

This path continues the Hermetic ray of the caduceus: it is the path of inner teachings. All experiences we have of inner wisdom and learning are from this path. The tarot trump assigned here is

THE HERMIT.

extremely appropriate: the Hermit, who can be a profound teacher. He also represents hidden potential—light hiding under a bushel.

This is the stage that holds the key to any further movement up the ladder. The 17th century English poet John Donne said, "No man is an island," meaning we can only function as a community. However, we need to be like an island sometimes; we need periods of isolation to take stock and think over our journey so far. At times of quiet contemplation, when we least expect it, a gentle inner voice whispers to us and shows us the way onward. From this stage on, we cannot continue without help or company. That company may seem to be on the outside, and it may seem to be on the inside: it matters not.

Hebrew Letter
Yod, the Hand

This letter represents a hand held out in peace and friendship. It is the hand of the Hermit in the tarot trump, holding out the light for us to better see the way ahead.

VISUALIZATION THE INNER GUIDE

Meeting your inner guide opens the way to learning and wisdom by helping you to understand more about your spiritual journey.

1   After relaxing and centering, find yourself back in your Garden of Consciousness, and go and sit in your "at home" place.

2   Go out once again through the opening, and this time take a path that you have not noticed before, which leads eastward toward some high mountains. The path leads to the very top of the very highest mountain.

3   The path may be long or short, wide or narrow, but know that you are ready now to walk it, and will not falter.

4   Just as you reach sight of the very top, you see a figure walking down toward you, welcoming you. This is your inner guide. As you meet, you can feel the warmth and goodness of this being enclose you.

5   Travel the rest of the way to the top of the mountain with your guide. Enjoy the magnificent view, and listen to everything that your guide tells you about the landscape. There will be many things you wish to ask your guide, about the path you have walked through your life so far, and about the journey to come. Ask your questions now.

6   Your guide gives you a gift and tells you that at any time, if you need to feel warmth and protection, just remember the gift and you will sense the same guiding presence.

7   At some point, you will know it is time to leave. Thank your guide, and retrace your steps back to your garden.

CHAPTER 5

Briah, World of Mind

Briah is the realm of the higher self, as distinct from the ego. It is the level at which we are truly conscious. Usually, the true self of Briah functions in the unconscious. It can send us messages "through the Veil," by putting experiences in our path or by sending us dreams. Once we start to operate from Briah, we can see far more clearly and gain more control of our lives.

This chapter looks at the seven stages of Briah—19 to 14—that together build the lower face of the Briatic tree. Once more, each section covers one stage, under the headings Ladder, describing the sephira it represents on the Ladder of Light; Tree, describing the path it represents on the Tree of Life; and Meditation, which suggests some mind work—another way to experience this stage.

Just like the other worlds, the lower face of Briah may be experienced in different ways. As the realm of the archangels, it describes the workings of the higher mind, and the interaction with these great beings of light. Overlaying the upper face of Yetzirah (the psychological world), Briah teaches us about the patterns behind the flows of our feeling. The angels in Yetzirah are the movers of the psyche, receiving their directions from the archangels of Briah.

Unlike angels, the archangels are named individually. Some of these names will be familiar

The Angel Michael Binding Satan—*"He cast him into the Bottomless Pit, and shut him up."* For the artist William Blake (1757–1827) the spiritual world was a reality; visitors from there regularly came to inspire him.

from the Old and New Testaments: Gabriel, Raphael, and Michael. Others are more unusual: Metatron and Sandalphon. These two names are both of Greek derivation: Sandalphon, the archangel of Malkuth, is described as being enormously tall, and tradition tells us that he is actually the same being as Metatron, the archangel of Kether.

The Work

G. I. Gurdjieff (1875–1949) was an enigmatic figure from Central Asia whose teachings ("The Work") are still extremely influential today. He believed that we are "asleep," and that we are fragmented beings. Most of the time we are on automatic pilot, simply reacting to our environment. Whenever some external event comes along that might awaken us, we switch across to another fragment of personality. "The Work," then, is to make a real I, so we can be truly, continuously awake in the world. These ideas closely parallel the relation between Yetzirah and Briah. When our awareness is focused on the realm of the psyche, we are completely at its mercy.

G. I. Gurdjieff: his teachings influence us to this day.

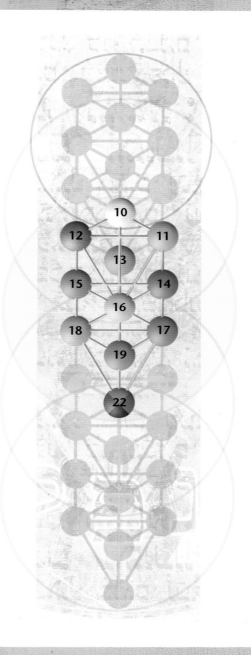

Stage 19 The Mind of Gabriel

In traditional Christian teaching Gabriel, the archangel of Yesod, is the angel who tells Mary that she has been chosen to be the Mother of Christ. In this role of messenger he is often represented carrying a trumpet. The literal translation of the name is "Strong One of God"—and the trumpet was originally a horn of fertility. Gabriel represents fecundity, the power of reproduction—giving an interesting slant on the New Testament story!

Ladder *Yesod in Briah, Da'ath in Yetzirah*

Moving up the ladder to this stage means moving out of the constraints of the everyday mind. Yesod in Briah brings a conscious knowledge of the psyche and the psychic realms: this is the highest point that Yetziratic consciousness may reach. In order to progress further up the ladder, what is required is a life built on new foundations: the foundations of total honesty.

Tree *Geburah to Chesed*

This path is the second to directly link the opposing pillars of force and form (see page 30). The experience of this path is meeting with the dark side of the self: what is known in Jungian psychology as "the shadow." All the things that we do not like in ourselves, we drop into the Abyss of Yetzirah, in order for it to be experienced in the outside world. Many teachings speak of "experiencing who we are through what we experience."

Life is a mirror that we hold up to ourselves. This stage is about accepting that fact, and facing the dark image in the mirror of life for what it truly is: our self. It needs great strength to face the dark twin, but we have powerful allies here to help us.

The tarot trump of this path echoes the power aspect: it is Strength. It shows a female figure holding open—or closed—the jaws of a lion. There is no sign of a struggle: there is perfect harmony between the woman and the lion. This is the gift of this path: once the dark twin is faced and re-integrated, the lower worlds of Yetzirah and Assiah no longer hold anything to fear: now we are the true master.

Hebrew Letter
Teth—the Snake

There are two sides to the snake. On one side he is the great teacher of humanity, bringing great wisdom. On the other he is Samiel, the dark twin, the snake who tempted Adam and Eve in Eden. In Christian Cabala, stage 19 represents the stage reached by an individual qualified to hold the office of subdeacon. The duties of a subdeacon are to present the chalice and paten at the Offertory, pour water into the wine for the Eucharist, and read from the Gospels.

Here we lose the constraints of the everyday mind and confront our psyche.

VIII

STRENGTH.

MEDITATION MEETING THE SHADOW

This meditation introduces you to the dark side of your self, to the dark twin. It will help you to understand how your experience of other people is formed by facets of your own self.

1. After relaxing and centering, find yourself back in your garden, in your "at home" place. Have your journal with you. This exercise should last no more than 20 minutes.

2. Call upon your inner guide by thinking of the gift he or she gave you up on the mountain (stage 20).

3. Bring to mind an individual in your life who is either an open enemy, or someone you find really difficult, or just a person who is totally different from you. Think what it is about this person that you find so difficult.

4. Call out to this person: ask an image of the person to appear. Do not censor your experience. The image that comes may be that person, but it may look just like you, or an animal or a cloud, or may be a completely abstract figure.

5. Welcome the figure in exactly the same way that you welcomed the image of your inner child (stage 24)—this image is just as much a part of you as your child.

6. With the help of your guide if required, interact with this person, until the 20 minutes is up. Then thank the figure and ask it to leave the garden. Thank your guide, and ask the guide to leave.

This meditation can be repeated many times, with more than one person if you wish. Each time it will become deeper and more profound. Also, watch what happens in your life: after all, you are now working directly with the causative factor of a lot of the things "out there." Something is bound to change.

Stage 18 The Mind of Raphael

This stage brings the experience of wholeness, of drawing together the strands of mind, body, and soul. Raphael, the archangel of Hod, is the archangel of healing—of "making whole." Illness arises from imbalance: healing is the process of bringing the system back into balance, so that everything works as a whole once more.

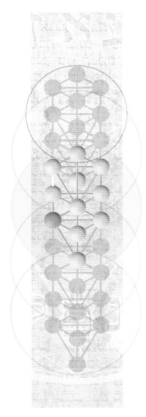

At this stage, we unite our mind with our body and soul.

Ladder *Hod in Briah, Binah in Yetzirah*

The function of Raphael is identical to that of a physician who, with a clear eye and steady hand, can analyze and measure all the different aspects of the problem, and then issue the instructions that will restore balance.

The Angels of Binah are the Aralim. The name can be translated as "Valiant Ones" or "Thrones." A throne is not an ordinary chair: it is a chair that holds not only a monarch, but a monarch's power. The thrones are repositories of the wisdom of Chockmah: they create the containers in which psychological insight can be held.

Tree *Geburah to Binah*

This path is the first path to cross the Abyss. It represents the power of Geburah (severity) focused and channeled by the understanding of Binah. When we are children, we do not have the experience to know right and wrong, so our parents provide this guidance. As we grow older, we internalize these guidelines into our psyche, so we grow up knowing that something is wrong, but not

THE CHARIOT.

even thinking about why, or from where we learned this.

This internalization of the parental limits is what Freudian psychologists refer to as the id. It works in the same way as the tarot trump that is associated with this stage: the Chariot.

Just as the charioteer controls the direction of the chariot, but the reins are invisible, so the control of the id is equally invisible to us. However, once we have a clear and honest view of ourselves, the chariot has another level of meaning. It represents the ability of our thoughts and feelings, symbolized by the two animals drawing the chariot, to work in perfect harmony—this means, without us having to use the reins.

Hebrew Letter

Cheth, the Fence

The fence is created in early life, by parents and guardians—it protects and helps to form young minds. In a deeper sense, it also represents the presence of God, in the sense that God is considered to be hovering over creation but not quite touching it.

MEDITATION TAKE CHARGE OF YOUR LIFE

This meditation can be done from within your Garden of Consciousness.

1. Think about a situation that right now is stopping you from moving on in your life. It might be lack of money, not enough help with work, not enough time, not enough love—whatever.
2. Think about how your life would be different if you had this thing. What would change? In your mind, visualize your life with this thing in it. Make it as complete and as positive as you can. Enjoy the experience of having it.
3. Now think of all the reasons why you cannot have what you want! For each reason, visualize a form for it, just as you did for your inner child at stage 24.
4. When you have all the reasons, lined up in front of you in your mind's eye, picture them shrinking and solidifying, until each one is a bright, shiny housebrick. Then take your bricks and build a solid brick wall around one area of your garden. (If there are not enough bricks, there are bound to be more reasons why you cannot have what you want. Think of these to make more bricks.) This bricked-in area is the home for the new thing that is now coming into your life.

You can now continue to build this little area in your garden with whatever materials come to hand: negative thoughts, such as "this will never work—what a ridiculous idea it is," make excellent bricks. This wall can be used again at stage 16.

Stage 17 The Mind of Haniel

This stage can be seen as both the source of love, of unity, and as the source of separation, of being marked out. The Archangel of Netzach is Haniel (Love of God), who has several alternative names, including Auriel (Light of God) and Phanael (Face of God). As Haniel, her function is to seal the love of humanity and God.

Here we are singled out for the experience of love and unity.

Ladder Netzach in Briah, Chockmah in Yetzirah

Phanael was the archangel who, in the book of Job, wrestled with and lamed Job. This was a "marking out"—Job was marked by God as one of his own. The meaning of this laming would have been more obvious in pastoral societies, familiar with the idea of a King Breeder. The best male sheep in the flock were lamed, so that they could not run away, but instead concentrate on what the shepherd wanted from them: breeding. In our own lives, we sometimes need to be "lamed" so that our minds (Briah) become solely focused (Netzach) on our true expression (Yetzirah) of creativity (Chockmah).

Tree Tiphareth to Binah

The experience of this path is the experience of "unity through joy": the imagination of Tiphareth is brought to bear on the archetypal forms of Binah. What then occurs is the blossoming of Tiphareth, into the Love of God. Such an intense experience of the divine would seem to be far from commonplace, but in fact this is a fairly familiar experience, as is made clear by the Tarot trump of this path, the Lovers.

Falling in love, as anyone who has gone through it will know, is an exhilarating, consciousness-raising, life-changing experience. People will do extraordinary things, perform extreme sacrifices, in the name of love. It has been described as a divine madness, and rightly so, for when we are in that state, we are touching the energies of the 17th stage.

There has been a long tradition of poets describing their love of God in terms of love of the lover. The *Song of Songs* in the Old Testament is a fine example of this; other examples are the Hindu princess Mirabai and the Sufi Rumi.

Sufism has a strong tradition of poetry to The Beloved—meaning God. This teaches that, unless we choose to walk the middle pillar of a direct relationship with God, we can find God only through others. Mitzvah is a very important Kabbalistic teaching here: service to others. To find God, reach out to others.

Hebrew Letter
Zayin—the Sword

The letter Zayin indicates another aspect of this stage: the fact that ultimately, all separation, all duality, has been created from a more fundamental truth. God/humankind, man/woman: any duality is actually a divided unity—and the sword is the ultimate instrument of division. Beyond this stage, such divisions become less and less important.

MEDITATION REACHING OUT TO OTHERS

This meditation can be done from within your Garden of Consciousness. It should take about 20 minutes.

1. Bring to mind an individual who is significant in your life: your spouse or partner, someone you love or have loved, a close friend, or just a person whom you admire. Think what it is about this person that you find attractive.

2. As with meeting the shadow (stage 19), call out to this person: ask an image of the person to appear.

3. Welcome the figure in exactly the same way that you welcomed the image of your inner child (stage 24)—this image is as much a part of you as your inner child is.

4. With the help of your guide if required, interact with the image until the 20 minutes is up. Then thank the figure and ask it to leave the garden. Thank your guide and ask the guide to leave.

At other times you can call up the image of another person whom you like, love, and admire. It is good to perform this meditation more than once, using as many people as you can think of.
At this stage of mind, all duality is illusion. The inner child is a part of the whole person. The shadow is a part of the whole person. The people to whom you feel attracted are a part of the whole person. The qualities that you love, respect, and admire in others are qualities that you have in yourself—maybe obviously, maybe hiding very deep down. But if they were not a part of you, they would not call out to you in others. The mirror of life shows us the very best of ourselves, as well as sometimes the very worst.

Stage 16 The Mind of Michael

The consciousness of this stage is like the exhilaration that can be occasionally experienced when standing on a high place, overlooking an amazing view. It is that "king of the world" feeling, that mountains could be moved just by saying the word. When experiencing life from this place, we feel an extraordinary sense of calm and centeredness.

Here we are centered and calm as higher energies are channeled through us and communicated to others.

THE HIEROPHANT

Ladder *Malkuth in Atziluth, Tiphareth in Briah, Kether in Yetzirah*

This, the second stage to exist in three worlds, is like a king-pin, around which the rest of the ladder revolves: 16 is half of 32, and the Tiphareth of Briah is the middle sephira of the middle world. It is the center (Tiphareth) of paradise (Briah), where the Tree of Knowledge of good and evil grows. This stage is also the kingdom (Malkuth) of heaven (Atziluth) and the crown (Kether) of consciousness (Yetzirah).

The archangel of Tiphareth is Michael, the shining bright one. He is seen as the representative of God to humankind—his name means "similar to God." Places that have a lot of light, especially the tops of hills, are dedicated to Michael. Many hill churches are named after St. Michael; the Church constructed buildings on sites that were existing, pagan places of worship. The most famous of these in Europe are St. Michael's chapel on the top of the Tor at Glastonbury in England, and Mont-Saint-Michel in France.

Tree *Chesed to Chockmah*

This path crosses the Abyss upon the active pillar, the pillar of force. To be conscious at this stage is to experience the channeling of higher energies, transforming them to make them real and meaningful to others below. The tarot trump of this path, the Hierophant, symbolizes this. He is the link between the world of God and the world of humankind. Through him spiritual power moves down into the lower worlds.

In medieval tarot packs, this card is called the Pope. In the Roman Church, the Pope speaks for God on earth. When he speaks *ex-cathedra*, he speaks not as himself, but as a mouthpiece for the wisdom (Chockmah) of God, expressing God's love (Chesed). The challenge of this stage is to be our own heirophants, channeling that spiritual power for ourselves and for the others around us.

Hebrew Letter *Vau—the Nail*

This nail is like the omphalos, the stone that, in Greek myth, marked the center of the world. When the nail is fixed in, everything can move around it like a catherine wheel. The awareness represented by this stage is the true fixed point of consciousness: the still, small voice at the core of our being that is often lost amid the business (busy-ness) of life. In Christian Cabala, the priest symbolizes the 16th stage.

MEDITATION I AM THAT I AM

The intention of previous meditations has been to give clearer answers to the question, "Who am I?" This exercise pulls these answers all together. This meditation can be done from within your inner garden.

1   When you are feeling at peace, start to think about what you have learnt about yourself, over the life that you have lived so far. View your life rather like a movie, with someone else, an actor, playing the central role. Observe the ups and the downs of your life with interest, but also with the detachment that is possible when watching movies.

2   Now recall the experiences you have had in your Garden of Consciousness, plus any other experiences you have had that have helped to show you the inner you. What did your meeting with the inner child tell you? What about the meeting with your physical, emotional, and mental selves as figures symbolizing your body, feelings, and thoughts? The meeting with your inner guide? The shadow? Your loved and respected ones? Remember what happened, but also maintain the detachment that is possible when recalling experiences.

3   As you watch your life-movie, and as you recall your inner experiences, remember that there is someone watching, someone recalling. That someone is the stillness at the center, the point around which everything else is whirling. As you continue to watch and recall, get a sense of that stillness in you. Realize that wherever you are, and whatever you do, it is all whirling around. And it is all whirling around this central point, the stillness at the center, that is you.

4   If you like, and if you have done the Take Charge of Your Life meditation (stage 18), feel that this stillness at the core of your being is centered on the walled area in your inner garden.

Stage 15   The Mind of Khamael

The archangel of Geburah is Khamael, or Sammael, meaning "He who sees God." This stage represents the ability to focus on one thing to the exclusion of all others, and the breakthrough to which such a focus can lead. Khamael was the archangel who had such dedication to and focus on God, that he refused to acknowledge God's creation, humanity.

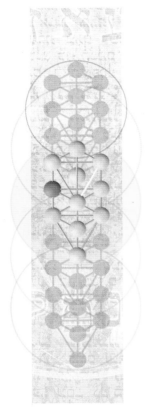

At this stage, sudden changes of fortune may bring profound but necessary changes of consciousness.

Ladder   Geburah in Briah

Just as the Seraphim—the angels of Geburah—will burn away all parts of the psyche that are unnecessary, so Khamael will remove any thoughts that distract us from the path of return, if we open ourselves fully to his energy. Of course this, as with all the other stages, is working right here right now in our lives. Khamael will remove obstacles on our path even when we do not realize that they are obstacles. This includes jobs, relationships, homes—anything! Understandably, if we remain unaware of his work, such removals can come as a bit of a shock! Khamael's work brings about profound changes of consciousness through sudden changes in fortune, which will be seen as being absolutely right and absolutely beneficial only years or even decades later. At the time they can seem to be more of the devil's work!

Tree   Tiphareth to Chockmah

If Khamael is left to do his work correctly, in time there will be illumination, a breakthrough of consciousness. This is the "Ah" moment of seeing

THE EMPEROR.

inside a Zen koan (riddle), or Archimedes' "Eureka" experience. The energy and exhilaration is released at Chockmah (wisdom) and rushes down this path into consciousness at Tiphareth (balance). The power experienced here is perfectly symbolized in the Emperor, the tarot trump for this path. The Emperor represents the highest expression of God's will on Earth, and is the ultimate source of temporal power.

In Christian Cabala the 15th stage is symbolized by the paten (plate) which holds the consecrated bread—the body of Christ—during the Mass.

Hebrew Letter

Heh, the Window

A window is a small opening that allows a portion of daylight into a room. In a similar way, this stage allows a specific part of the will of God to shine into our lives, illuminating our consciousness. Just as every window has a unique view, we all have our own view of God, our own path up the ladder.

MEDITATION LETTING GO OF BAGGAGE

It is often difficult to know the right direction to take in life. It may be because life is cluttered with relationships, habits, or possessions that have now been outgrown. When you cannot see the wood for the trees, it is time to start cutting down a few trees!

1. This meditation can be done from within your inner garden. When you are feeling at peace, think again about all you have learned about yourself. Be aware of the still, small voice at the core of your being. From this place of stillness, watch the facets of your life flowing around you.

2. You will notice one facet that does not flow with the other parts. Examine it more closely; you will notice that it adds little of benefit to your life, or takes away far more than it gives.

3. Acknowledge to yourself the benefit in your life that this part once played, and that the benefit is now complete: this aspect is unnecessary, and needs to be removed.

Once you have identified such an element of your life, using the meditation above, you will find that circumstances will come together to remove it. If it is no longer of any benefit, simply focusing on it is enough to activate the function of Khamael. If your life does not conflict in this way, you are ready to move on to the next part of the meditation: Finding the Path.

FINDING THE PATH

As work on the inner life continues, the outer life will change too. Situations that were seemingly stuck will miraculously unstick. New challenges and opportunities arise, often totally unexpectedly. If the work continues, focus especially on the I Am That I Am meditation, and the path will emerge, maybe with trumpets blaring, maybe without you fully understanding it.

Stage 14: The Mind of Tzadkiel

This stage brings about the resolution of contradictions. The resolution releases much energy that can then be used to move forward in life. The name "Tzadkiel" means "Justice of God." His energy gives an ability to perceive many different things at the same time—in contrast to Khamael, who focuses on a single thing.

Here we understand the reason for painful experiences and are then able to move forward in life.

Ladder Chesed in Briah

Tzadkiel's energy lets us hold in our mind and weigh up several factors when judging a situation, so that we can come to a better decision. It also gives us the open-mindedness required when trying to understand what can be experienced as the harshness of Khamael.

There is always a reason behind any kind of unpleasant experience we might have to endure: when we reach this stage of consciousness, we are able to see what those reasons are. Often, the factors to be considered seem to be diametrically opposed. Tzadkiel's gift is to show the ways in which seemingly irreconcilable ideas can be united in perfect harmony.

This idea is also expressed in the form of the Empress tarot card. It shows a beautiful mature woman seated on cushions in a cornfield. Traditionally, this woman is the Earth Mother—ever-pregnant, ever-virginal, joyful, and sorrowful at the same time.

Such contradiction is the essence of this stage. Those parts of ourselves that we most despise are our greatest strengths. In our most feared weaknesses lie our greatest talents. Each is the seed of the other. We come to the essence of this stage when we are learning to embrace such contradictions as just two sides of the same coin.

Tree Binah to Chockmah

The 14th path is the path joining Binah and Chockmah: it therefore represents the ultimate union of opposites. This path also has connotations of Da'ath, the non-sephira that sits across the Abyss between them.

In Christian Cabala the 14th stage is the chalice, which during the Mass holds the consecrated wine—the blood of Christ. The chalice is also the Holy Grail, traditionally the actual cup that was used at the Last Supper, and a very important part of Arthurian Legend. This is a reminder of the ultimate goal of this climb up the ladder: the quest to find the Holy Grail is realized at stage 10, when the Grail is placed on the high altar.

Hebrew Letter
Daleth—the Door
This is the door to the House of God. It is possible to go two ways through a door: the experience of each is very different—diametrically opposed, in fact. But the door is the same door. Daleth also represents the poor man. This derives in part from the shape of the letter, which looks like a person bent over. It reflects how we need to be in order to progress along this path: "the meek shall inherit the earth."

EXERCISE AFFIRMATIONS

Once the center of our being is found and the direction in which we are heading is known, we need to just get on and head there. But often what is lacking is the energy and excitement that says, "Yes, I want this to happen." This straightforward exercise will start to provide that energy.

1. Start with a simple affirmation: "I feel good." Say it, out loud, like you mean it, then say it some more. (You do not have to feel good to say that you feel good. You can lie.)
2. Notice your reactions to saying this. They may range from embarrassment to exhilaration. Then say it some more.
3. After only a few repetitions, you will start to feel good. You have changed your life! Once you know that saying something can actually change where you are in yourself, you can start to choose affirmations that are relevant to your own situation in life.
4. Think about the direction you want your life to take.
5. Decide how you want to be in that situation. Picture what it will be like.
6. Now imagine that you have arrived at the place you want to be. What is it like? Make as clear a picture in your mind as you possibly can.
7. Now create a simple, positive phrase that describes all, or a significant part, of your experience, in the present tense. For example "I am now enjoying presenting my first paper to the Society," or "I am happily relaxing in the garden with my partner and three children around me."
8. Say this as you said, "I feel good." Repeat it on a regular basis for at least a week.

Remember: when you start to say an affirmation it will seem like it isn't true. But that can change, if you want it to.

CHAPTER 6

Atziluth, World of Insight

In translation, Atziluth means "emanation," or an emergence from nothing. It is the process by which nothing becomes something, but comes before creation. The gods of each of the sephiroth are an emanation from the One God of Adam Kadmon: an aspect of Him. These gods are immensely significant in our lives, as the originators of everything that is contained in them.

The previous moves from world to world are part of everyday life. The change from the physical experience of Assiah to the psychological consciousness of Yetzirah, and from there on to the mind of Briah, is familiar to all.

The next stage on the journey up the ladder moves beyond the mind, into the realm of insight and archetype, the world of Atziluth. This transition is usually less well known: yet living in this world is just as much a part of our birthright as having a well-functioning body, a balanced emotional life, and an inquiring intellect.

For as long as an individual has a body, the spiritual world will be experienced as part of the "next stage": something bigger than themselves. In the journey up the ladder, whenever some goal is achieved, there is always something more to be gained. Until perfection is reached, Atziluth is always beyond what has just been attained. The closest anyone can

Light appearing in the darkness—illustration by Robert Fludd in the Utriusque Cosmi, *Vol.1, Oppenheim, 1617. As the Zohar explains: "When the secret of secrets wished to reveal himself, he began to produce a point of light. Before that point broke through and became apparent, the infinite (en soph) was entirely hidden and radiated no light."*

Living together in a community is the closest people come to an experience of the transcendent. Moses receives the Ten Commandments for the Israelites.

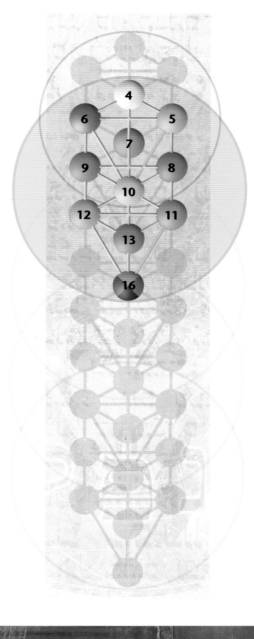

come to an experience of the transcendent is in the collective experience of the community.

In the Western world in times past, the divine force was part of everyday life. Living in a simpler way, the spiritual was a communal experience: shared within the extended family, the tribe, and society. Now a more complex lifestyle has forced most people's focus to shift from the community to themselves, and in many cities of the West, society consists of a loose-knit collection of individuals. As a result of the loss of real community, much contact with the spiritual has been lost. Until people find a way to refocus their lives on something beyond themselves, Atziluth will be an unknown experience.

Three stages are described here: the sephiroth of Atziluth from Yesod to Netzach, at the edge of the Atziluthic Veil. Stage 10, the Tiphareth of Atziluth, is where God and Man meet. It is described in Chapter 7, which covers Adam Kadmon.

Stage 13 The Insight of Chaddai el Chai

The 13th stage shifts consciousness into Atziluth, the realm beyond creation—for creation starts at Briah. Atziluth is the life above the Abyss, which humanity experiences through the spiritual senses of intuition and inspiration.

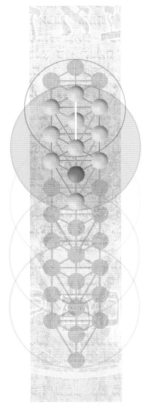

Here, we must balance wisdom and understanding—and need determination to succeed.

From here upward, there are no words that can fully describe the experience of any of the stages. Everything that is written about this and all following stages should therefore be taken as allegory and allusion, and ultimately untrue, in that the process of writing has converted it into the experience of different worlds (those of Yetzirah and Briah).

Ladder *Yesod in Atziluth, Da'ath in Briah*

The God-name of Yesod is Chaddai el Chai, meaning Lord/Lady of Life. There are connotations of both masculine and feminine energies here. Here we meet the highest expression of the union of opposites: beyond this point, on the middle pillar, polarity is no more. The expression of God at this stage is directly concerned with the emanation of life, and the energy flows directly into the knowledge (Da'ath) of creation (Briah). Here is the Divine of Atziluth, who pushes his own image through onto the creation of Briah.

Tree *Tiphareth to Kether*

This path crosses the Abyss and takes consciousness into the realm of the Crown for the first time. The quality of experience is like making a long journey, which is straightforward at first, but which becomes increasingly arduous until it is virtually

impossible. Any deviation from the path causes the journey to end in failure. Failure is also possible because the path disappears. The goal is finally reached only through perseverance and sheer bloody-mindedness. Deviating from the path draws you to one or the other pillar, and ultimately creates a drop into the Abyss, and hopefully, a return to the start. The way to walk this path is symbolized by the tarot trump of the Priestess. This is the last tarot card on the middle pillar. It shows the Priestess sitting between the two pillars of force and form. At her feet is the crescent moon of Yesod in Atziluth. At her breast is an equal-armed cross. She carries a scroll which shows the letters "TORA." This means teaching. The message is that only by exercising an iron will and a balance of wisdom and understanding can this journey be made successfully.

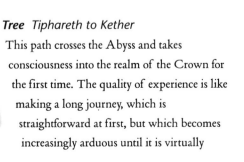

Hebrew Letter *Gimel—the Camel*

A camel can cross vast distances of desert without requiring food or water. This is the quality of inner resources needed to cross the Abyss, traveling from the mental world of Briah into the spiritual light of Atziluth. The form of the letter Gimel traditionally is that of a rich man running after a poor man in order to give him charity. This represents the freedom of choice available to do good in the world, to make a self-sacrifice so that others may benefit.

SYMBOLISM OF THE CROSS

In the Christian Cabala, this stage is represented by the Cross in the middle of the altar. The cross is an extremely ancient symbol—far older than Christianity. It is the meeting of the horizontal and the vertical, representing the balance of two fundamentally different energies: masculine and feminine, yin and yang. The most common form of cross in ancient symbolism was the equal-armed cross, the cross of matter, where the energies have come together to create the four elements of material existence.

The Christian Cross has an extended bottom piece. This implies the balance of energies is occurring at one level, and then flowing down to another level, for example, the sacrifice of Jesus Christ, who represents God-made-Man, who sacrificed himself in the world of matter. It is therefore a perfect symbol for the Christian sacrament of Holy Communion, which represents this sacrifice. The 13th stage symbolizes the stage of the priesthood.

Stage 12 The Insight of Elohim Tzabaoth

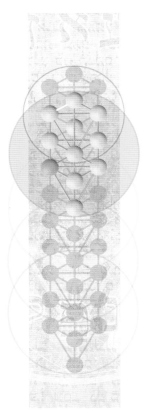

Several names for God are used in the Old Testament: Elohim *is one—the root* El *in Hebrew means goddess, but* ∕im *is the Hebrew ending for words that are masculine plural. Tzabaoth means hosts, or armies. The insight brought by this goddess of Hod lets us respond to situations that have been created by wrong actions. At Stage 12 we are able to understand our actions clearly and objectively, analyze the current state of affairs, and then act again to change the situation for the better.*

Looking at ourselves clearly and objectively, we can learn to take responsibility for our actions.

Ladder *Hod in Atziluth, Binah in Briah*

The archangel of Binah, Tzaphkiel, is known as the "Keeper of the Records of Evolution." He is seen as a dark angel, and he and Ratziel, the bright archangel of Chockmah, have been portrayed as the two angels standing on either side of an individual: one evil, the other good. In fact, Tzaphkiel's task is to record everything that occurs in the world.

This function is to do with the workings of karma in an individual's life. It is far easier, when an individual has done something wrong, to put the blame for the act on something, anything else. Traditionally, then, blame was taken by the evil angel: the being that has noted and recorded it. But if people can accept responsibility for their actions, they can do something about the wrong they have done, and therefore they work on their karma.

Tree *Binah to Kether*
This is the path linked with the clairvoyant. At the level of this path on the tree, consciousness is beyond

time. So any glimpse into this level of reality is going to show past, present, and future as one eternal Now. Experiencing this is far easier than bringing back the information in one sensible piece.

• Absorbing the information as a consciousness within time brings it into Briah (the mental world).

•Turning it into images in the mind moves it into Yetzirah (the psychological world) and the∕here∕and∕now.

• Communicating it to another changes it into the concrete terms of Assiah (the physical world). Each step takes a little more from the actual experience. No wonder much genuine clairvoyance ends up as the illusion and wish∕fulfillment of lower consciousness.

This stage rarely functions as it should, but when it does, the individual will seem to have magical powers of insight and intuition.

The Tarot trump of this path is the Magus or Magician. This is the last trump on the Hermetic teaching path. It therefore sums up the journey that the orange ray of the mind takes. The Magus has complete insight (Atziluth) into his thoughts (Hod), and can therefore understand and control (Binah) his mind (Briah). This lets him also control his emotions and his body. This control is symbolized by the objects that lay on the table in front of him: the coin, cup, sword, and staff represent the four elements.

The reason he has such control and insight is two-fold:

- He understands he is here as a gift of the gods, and he serves a force beyond himself: "not my will, Lord, but thine." Indicating this, he points the wand in his right hand up to the heavens.
- He knows that the only place that he can actually do any good is on the material plane,

Assiah—for example, in his workplace, in his place of worship, in his home. Indicating this, he points his left hand down to the ground.

Hebrew Letter
Beth—the House

Beth is the first letter of the first word in the Bible— *be-Rashith* means "in the beginning." It is used to represent creation.

A house is a container for the household: consequently, Binah, the Great Mother, is considered to hold the creation of all of the lower worlds in her womb.

SYMBOLISM OF THE CONSECRATED BREAD

In Christian Cabala, the 12th stage represents the consecrated bread on the left side of the altar. This is the supreme sacrifice of Jesus Christ, who offered his life—his body—so that humankind could be saved.

Stage 11   The Insight of Jehovah Tzabaoth

Jehovah Tzabaoth is the God-name of Netzach. As in the God-name of stage 12, Hod in Atziluth, Tzabaoth means hosts, or armies. Jehovah, however, is a masculine form of God: the name therefore means Lord of Hosts. The insight of this God is that of joy and creativity: it is the feeling that sometimes comes when waking up on a summer's morning and feeling that everything is alright and that today there are thousands, millions of ways to express one's inner truth.

At this stage, we are joyful and experience the wisdom that comes from laughter.

Ladder *Netzach in Atziluth, Chockmah in Briah*

The archangel of Chockmah, Raziel, is traditionally the archangel who gave Adam the Book of Wisdom (Kabbalah) as he left the Orchard. This stage can therefore be seen as the ultimate source of this teaching. How refreshing to see the tarot trump of this stage: the Fool. It is easy to take everything too seriously; laughter is a great leveler and healer, and often the simplest things are not only funny, but truer than all the complex explanations, diagrams, and theories.

Tree *Chockmah to Kether*

The path between Kether (crown) and Chockmah (wisdom) is the first movement out from the Crown, as well as the last movement back into it. This is a path of simplicity, of pure energy, before any thought or action has arisen to complicate matters. It is an energy that is expressed perfectly in the tarot card The Fool.

This is the last trump card on the Orphic path of nature and ecstasy. It therefore sums up the journey that this green ray of passion takes. The Fool is dressed in a kilt that is covered in flowers and greenery, which makes him a representation of the ancient god of fertility known as the green man.

The three paths of the caduceus that go up the Ladder are the three available channels of contact with the divine. The two most familiar ones are as follows:

- The Mystic, walking the middle path straight up to the source, will be contacted by divinity through visions and his or her love of God.
- The Intellectual, walking the Hermetic path of mind, analysis, and contemplation, will be contacted by divinity through sudden illuminations and insight and his or her understanding of God.

The majority of humanity, however, is neither monk nor scientist, so the Orphic path is the most accessible one. Before the Industrial Revolution, most people lived in the countryside. They worked on the land, in tune with nature, using the products of the land to create tools and things of beauty. This intimate connection with the land meant they were more aware of life's rhythms, and had an innate wisdom about life and God.

Nature is not nearly so familiar to people of the modern Western world. Nature lovers will tend to experience it as tourists, not as a part of their life. Western culture is heavily oriented toward a mental appreciation of the world: most work is mental, not physical. Most leisure activity is passive, not active. So for many people, the easiest route to a relationship with divinity has been destroyed, leaving them godless.

Hebrew Letter
Aleph—the Ox

An Ox is immensely strong, and immensely stubborn. It is therefore a perfect symbol for the power that moves through this stage. The form of the Aleph is of two letter Yods, above and below a letter Vau. This represents the relationship between God and humanity, similar in essence but divided by the void.

SYMBOLISM OF THE CONSECRATED WINE

In Christian Cabala, the consecrated wine on the right side of the altar symbolizes this stage. Wine was also sacred in the Orphic Mysteries. The popular image of a drunken Bacchus/Dionysius—riding a donkey, drinking from a jug of wine, and enjoying himself immensely—is a distant echo of this once-powerful Mystery cult.

This stage is the last of the 22 stages that are of humanity. The next stage in sequence up the ladder is stage 10; this is where humanity finally meets God. The remaining stages (from 10 to 1) are the stages of God, of Adam Kadmon. These final 10 stages are explored in the next chapter.

CHAPTER 7

Adam Kadmon, the Archetypal World

This chapter looks at the 10 stages of the consciousness of Adam Kadmon, stepping down from stage 1 to meet Humanity at stage 10. Stage 10 also represents the individual spark of life. The next stage, stage 11, is the highest level of consciousness a person can reach and remain human—that is, stay in a physical body.

What does it mean to represent stages of consciousness that are beyond humanity? Another name for it is the archetypal consciousness or world. This chapter looks at the archetypal world in human terms, describing some early attempts to gain understanding of this through the Ten Commandments, brought down from the mountain by Moses. These commandments are often seen in a rather negative light, because they often insist: "thou shalt not." This chapter attempts to show the commandments in a different light. It also looks at some of the practices of the original Kabbalists, including their meditation techniques, and letter and number permutations.

The archetypal world is that of Adam Kadmon; that part of God which, according to Lurianic Kabbalah, limits itself so as to create a space into which Creation is poured, in His own image.

On Mount Sinai, Moses receives the Ten Commandments, a covenant between God and his people (Exodus 34: 1–10).

The Tree of Perfect Life

By definition the tree of the archetypal world is perfect: the Tree of Perfect Life. This is because for Adam Kadmon there has been no Fall, so there is no Abyss. The perfect tree's form is different to the trees of the imperfect world that have fallen into the Abyss of Atziluth (the Tree of Knowledge of good and evil). The perfect tree's outline is more symmetrical.

Mapping the perfect tree onto the Atziluthic Tree of Life is not straightforward; there are differences. For example, Tiphareth is above not below Geburah and Chesed; similarly, Yesod is above not below Netzach and Hod. Both trinities are perfect replicas of the three supernals at a lower level, rather than a reflection of them in the Abyss (in the perfect tree, the Abyss does not exist). These trinities are composed of the six sephiroth which, according to Lurianic Kabbalah, shattered during Sheviret HaKelim—the breaking of the vessels. For these six, therefore, the usual numerical sequence is awry.

The perfect tree of Adam Kadmon does not have the imagery of the tarot trumps and the letters of the Hebrew alphabet: these are human symbols, representing a human scale of experience that finish at stage 11. On the Kadmon tree at the top of this ladder are only the numbers 1 to 10. They represent a more archetypal, abstract experience: 2 + 2 will always equal 4. Other numbers form universal, unchanging patterns, and would be understood by any mathematician.

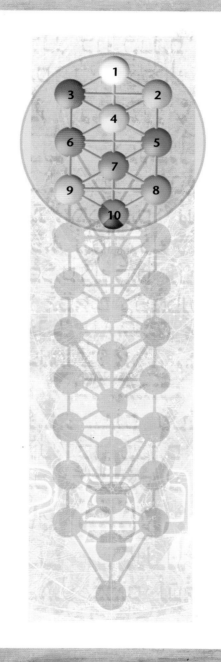

Archetype of the Supernals—Negative Existence

The First, Second and Third Commandments

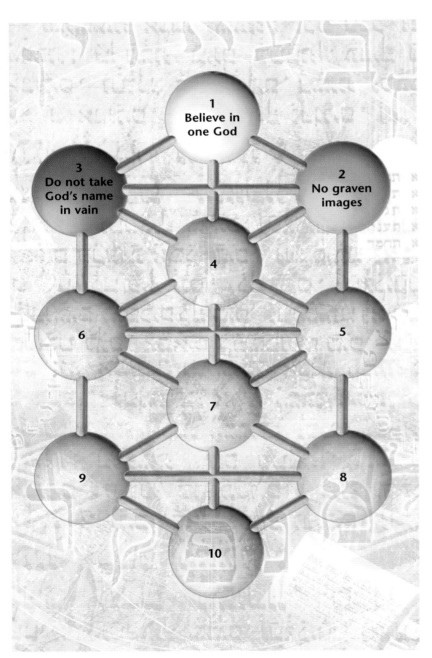

Western Mystery Qabalah describes the "three veils of negative existence," which are states of being that exist before the state of "I am" in Kether (see stage 4), and which exist above and beyond Kether on the Tree of Life. As Kether on a single tree represents the world of Atziluth, of emanation, the three veils can be seen as what is, before emanation: that is, they are another representation of Adam Kadmon.

The three veils are:

- AIN, meaning the state of nothingness, a void, an absence;
- AIN SOPH, meaning endless, boundless, infinity;
- AIN SOPH AUR, meaning limitless light.

They correspond to stages 1 to 3 on the ladder.

Stage 1 Archetype of One

The First Commandment
Believe in one God

At the time Moses brought the Commandments to the Israelites, many Gods were being worshiped: every nomadic tribe had their own set; there were gods of rivers and gods of mountains, sky gods and sea gods, home gods and family gods. The message Moses brought was that however many expressions there are of God, ultimately there is just one.

This first commandment sums up the essence of the Kabbalah. Although there are many gods—at least ten in each of the sephiroth of Atziluth, for example, the Kabbalist always knows that they are all expressions of the One. Moses' message, and the understanding of Kabbalah, is just as relevant to people today. The Western world has many Gods, although they are no longer described as such, among them the gods of science, of politics, of media and entertainment—each with their own pantheon—the "stars." It is important to remember that, although inspiration and goodness can come from many different sources, there is only one God.

Stage 2 Archetype of Two

The Second Commandment
No graven images

The map is not the terrain, the movie is not the reality—the graven image is not God. How easy it is to place faith in a substitute, especially if it looks great and sounds even better!

This commandment is connected with the Old Testament story of the golden calf. Moses came down from the mountain with the Ten Commandments and found the Israelites worshipping this. He had been gone for so long that they had lost faith, and had made the statue in order to worship it instead.

The essence of this teaching is that only a direct, inner relationship with God has any reality, because that is the only place where, ultimately, God exists. Everything else is a road sign, just pointing the way to God. The danger is that road signs can sometimes look so grand!

When we consider the great Master's teachings, the kindly priest, the Kabbalah, they can all become golden calves, or what might be called sacred cows, if we let them take that central place in our lives. Once that happens, the still, small voice inside gets swamped.

Stage 3 Archetype of Three

The Third Commandment
Do not take God's name in vain

The third commandment is hard to keep—it is sometimes easy to forget that swearing is taking God's name in vain!

This stage is the stage of Binah in Kadmon, whose virtue is silence. This may seem odd, especially in these times, when communication and the media have such importance. Speech is also extremely important in Kabbalah and the Judaeo-Christian tradition: the Gospel of John starts with "In the beginning was the Word," and in Genesis, God created everything through the power of speech. In many cultures, people are cautious about who knows their name, because of the belief that if someone knows your name, they have power over you. Salesmen know this: they will try to get the name of the person they are selling to as early as possible. The true name of God is also hidden: it is represented by four letters, Yod-Heh-Vau-Heh, but even these are never pronounced—they are represented by other names: Jehovah, or Tetragrammaton (meaning four-letter-name).

Names are important, and speech has power—and both can be abused. Aleister Crowley, the famous English magician and Qabalist, once said, "Every man and every woman is a Star." He meant that in everyone is an immortal spark of God, and that the spark is the person. Everything else is a creation of that spark. So, to truly keep the third commandment, it is necessary to speak to and about everybody with the same respect and honor that should also be accorded to God.

The Tetragrammaton represents the holy name of God and concentrates within itself the essence of creation. From Sephardi Bible, 1385.

Many divinities are worshiped throughout the world. These are all expressions of the true God, and they lead us toward the One.

Stage 4 Archetype of Four

The Fourth Commandment
Remember the Sabbath Day

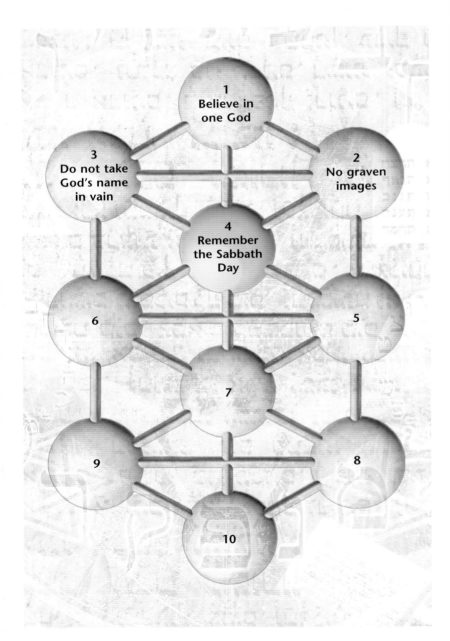

"And on the seventh day God ended his work" *(Genesis 2:2).* Garden of Delights *by Hieronymous Bosch (c.1450–1516).*

The fourth commandment is about keeping some time special. In the creation story of Genesis, the world is created in six days—six is the number of Tiphareth—and on the seventh day God rests. This has become an archetypal rhythm throughout the world: all modern cultures use a seven-fold pattern of days and weeks. For Jews, Saturday—the Sabbath—is holy, because as Saturn's day, it is the seventh and last day of the week. For Christians, Sunday is holy, because that was the day Jesus Christ rose from the dead. For Moslems, the holy day is Friday, as dictated by their holy book, the Koran. For most people, the weekly day of rest has lost its original meaning as a time to remember God and the inner quest. Other days are celebrated on an annual rhythm: birthdays, Easter, Thanksgiving, Hanukkah. These holy days (or holidays) are also very important, and can also serve as a reminder of the spiritual life.

Kether in Atziluth

The God of Atziluth (the spiritual world) is Eheiheh. It means "I am," and sums up all that is, was, or will be: it is a level of consciousness completely beyond time and space and is the first movement of emanation at the crown of the Atziluthic Tree of Life.

The best way to say the name Eheiheh is to have a good belly laugh. The sound of this laugh is a perfect expression of this ultimate level of being.

Archetype Chronos and Kairos

The mundane everyday life is a linear progression, starting at birth and ending at death. This is the life that most of us lead, most of the time. The Greeks called the type of time that this life is lived in "chronos," which is another name for Saturn, and the figure of Old Father Time.

There is also another type of time, called "Kairos." This is a far more subjective experience, where seconds can seem like hours and days like minutes. Kairos is also found in the rhythms of nature, of routine, and of regular sacred celebration.

There is an extraordinary quality of timelessness about doing something at the same time every week, or every year. Living in chronos, every minute is precious, because once it has gone it is lost forever, so we resent routine chores. Living occasionally in Kairos brings the realization that time is eternal, and with it comes a deep sense of peace and tranquility.

Hitbodedut Meditation

Meditation, or hitbodedut, was once central to Kabbalah. Its object was always to reach the level of consciousness where one could have a direct experience of God. Unlike many spiritual paths however, there was a very practical objective to this

beyond the illumination of the individual. The Kabbalist believed that the Jewish nation has a very specific task: to bring about the reunion of the Shekhinah and the Messiah, and thereby complete the process of Tikkun, or return.

Once a Kabbalist had achieved a certain level of consciousness, he became a living bridge between the two: there was always the possibility that he would be the one to make the final link. However, if he failed to maintain the bridge, the situation ultimately became worse than before: the Shekhinah and the Messiah ended up being even further apart.

Jewish folk tales are full of stories of rabbis who, through pride or ignorance, stopped the final wedding from taking place. For this reason, being a practicing Kabbalist was an extremely serious business: no-one trod the spiritual path lightly, because to embark on it was to take on an enormous amount of responsibility.

Saturn: his day (Saturday) is holy for Jews because it is the last day of the week.

Meditation and contemplation—as the approach of the mind—are fundamental to Kabbalah.

Stage 5 Archetype of Five

The Fifth Commandment
Honor thy Father and Mother

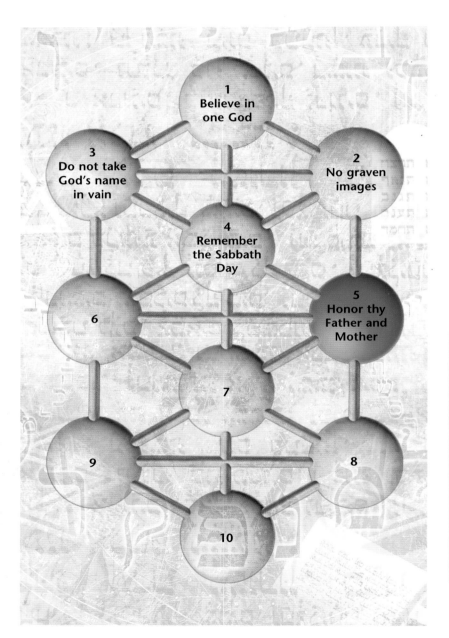

This commandment is associated with Chesed of Kadmon: obedience, another aspect of honor, is the virtue of Chesed. The meaning of this commandment was more accessible in former times, when generation gaps did not exist, and technology did not completely change people's lives every thirty years or so. For most of the time that humanity has been on this planet, a son's life was almost guaranteed to be like the life of his father, a daughter's life to be like that of her mother. So honoring your parents was honoring yourself, honoring what you were to become. Very few people in the West today are privileged enough to follow in their parent's footsteps on an external level. But on an inner level, nothing has changed.

At the archetypal level everything is perfect: nothing is left to chance. Therefore, when looking at an individual life, it can be nothing but perfect—even if at other levels it can feel rather different. As we grow up, our experiences of people shape our future life. All these experiences, at this level, are

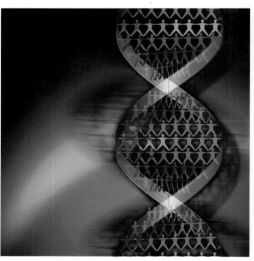

The double helix, the structure which carries the genes that we inherit and which makes us individual.

absolutely right and proper—because, at this level, we have chosen exactly these experiences. Parents are a perfect example: they give us the context into which we choose to be born. As archetypal images, they represent what is, and indicate the path that we have chosen to take in life. As physical people, their unique mix of nature and nurture shapes our path: parental genes and parental attitudes give a child the outlines of the life they will have. In addition, living in a more complex world, more complex things now contribute to the people we become: education, media, travel, and so on.

All the people that made up our childhood, and now make up our lives, should always be honored—not thought badly of or resented. They should be honored because, at this archetypal level, everybody is a spark of God, which we invite into our lives to teach us something.

Some people know exactly where they are going in their lives. This will be for one of two reasons. The most common is that one extremely strong part is dominating all the others and forcing a particular direction. The other is that all the different parts have lined up, and are all moving in the same direction: the inner conflicts have ceased. There is one other difference. It is impossible to "create" a part that is capable of dominating all others: people are either born with it or they are not. However, everyone can resolve their inner conflicts, eliminate any blocks, and line up the different parts.

Chockmah in Atziluth

The God-name of Chockmah (wisdom) is Jehovah, which is the name given to the four letters called the Tetragrammaton. These four letters also correspond with the four worlds of humankind that exist below Kadmon.

THE NAME OF GOD		
Letter	**World**	**Meaning**
Yod	Atziluth	Energy
Heh	Briah	Pattern
Vau	Yetzirah	Force
Heh	Assiah	Form

Writing the name of God out down the page gives the image of a person.

Tzeruf letter permutation

One extremely important method of meditation used by Kabbalists is letter permutations. Rabbi Abraham Abulafia, an influential Kabbalist from the 13th century, developed this technique. The technique uses as its starting point the letters of the most important name of God, the Tetragrammaton. The Kabbalist would shuffle the letters around, in a predetermined sequence—sometimes by writing them down, sometimes by memory—and then speak out the resulting words. Some of these words will have a meaning, others will not. However, all of these words are going to have the same numerical value (the Hebrew letters all have number values) which give them all the same essence. This leads to a deeper and deeper unveiling and understanding of God.

Obviously, this technique is going to have a deep effect only on those people who can read Hebrew, and, as a consequence, these days it has fallen for the most part into disuse.

From the Tetragrammaton flow the ten aspects of God, which correspond to the ten sephiroth.
From R. Fludd, Philosophia Sacra, *Frankfurt, 1626.*

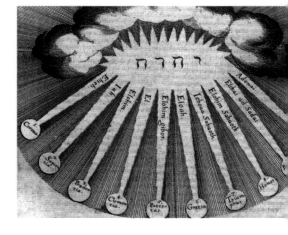

Stage 6 Archetype of Six

The Sixth Commandment
Thou shalt not kill

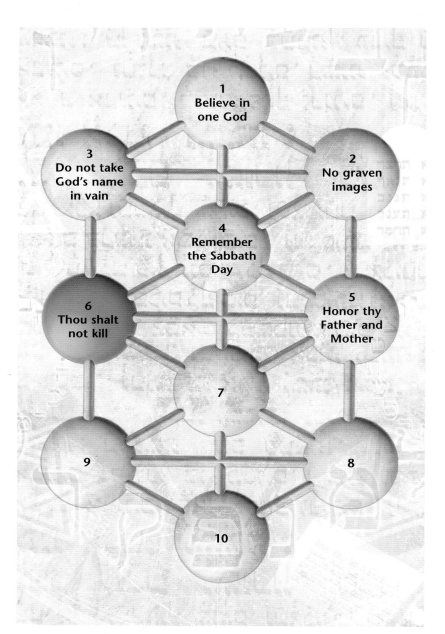

This corresponds to Geburah in Kadmon: Geburah is the sephira of Judgement. On an archetypal level, when one individual takes the life of another they will carry that action, weighed on their soul, until after their own death, at the time of Judgement. This is known, in Eastern traditions, as karma.

Of course, karma does not only accrue from such major actions as murder. In any action that "kills" a creation, when that action has been done from a place of imbalance, then the weight of the imbalance stays with the individual who performed the act. The greater the imbalance, the greater the karma—the weight carried by the soul. So a bed of roses that has been vandalized will accrue karma for the vandal. But the same action, cutting off the heads of the plants, when it is done by the gardener because it is time to prune them, has no karma attached to it at all, because the gardener is acting from a place of balance in himself.

The Wheel of Life shows how karma accrues for the individual depending on their actions and whether they act from a place of balance or imbalance.

Binah in Atziluth

The God-name of Binah (understanding) is Jehovah Elohim. The words are a mix of masculine and feminine, but in Kabbalah it is clear that the name should be translated as Goddess of Goddesses, or the Great Mother, for that is who she is.

The 22 letters of the Hebrew alphabet are divided up into three groups: the three mother letters first, then the seven doubles and finally the twelve singles. The three mothers are Aleph (Ah), Mem (Mm), and Shin (Shh), and they are associated with Binah, the Great Mother. To understand why three sounds are so fundamental, there is no need to look further than the cradle: they are the universal sounds made by mothers to their babies; sounds that transcend local variations in language.

Gematria Finding the Archetypal in the Mundane

One of the qualities of an archetype is that it has a universal meaning: it is true in whatever circumstances, at any time, and in any place. National laws are not archetypal: a traffic violation in Missouri will not stand up in a court in England. Language and customs are not archetypal: the greatest book in the English language will be meaningless in a country where English is not understood.

Mathematics has all the qualities of an archetype. The laws of number are universal—1+2 will always give the same answer as 2+1. Prime numbers—numbers that can be divided only by themselves and one—are the same wherever in the universe they are calculated. This is why numbers 1 to 10 are used to describe the world of Adam Kadmon: to give this sense of being beyond the limitations of time and space.

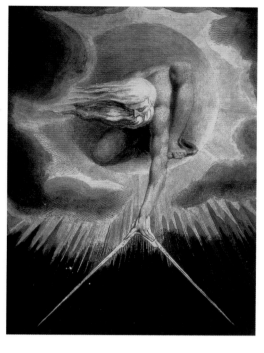

Divine geometry: this image of God using a compass indicates the close link Kabbalists see between numerical values and the divine.

In common with other early alphabets, each letter of the Hebrew alphabet has a numeric value: for example the first letter, Aleph, is 1, Beth is 2, and so on through the letters (see pages 124–125 for a table of these).

Kabbalists believed that calculating the numeric value of any word would demonstrate its archetypal essence, and that the same thing could be done for phrases. Any word or phrase that shares the same numeric value as another word or phrase will also share its essence.

When studying the books of the Old Testament, early Kabbalists searched for the hidden meaning that can be found there by looking for these numeric patterns. Much of the *Zohar* is a commentary on the early books of the Bible, describing some of these patterns. They were seen to be the revelation of God, and they do often reveal a hidden meaning in the words.

The three mother letters—Aleph, Mem, and Shin—whose sounds are common to all languages.

Stage 7 Archetype of Seven

The Seventh Commandment
Thou shalt not commit adultery

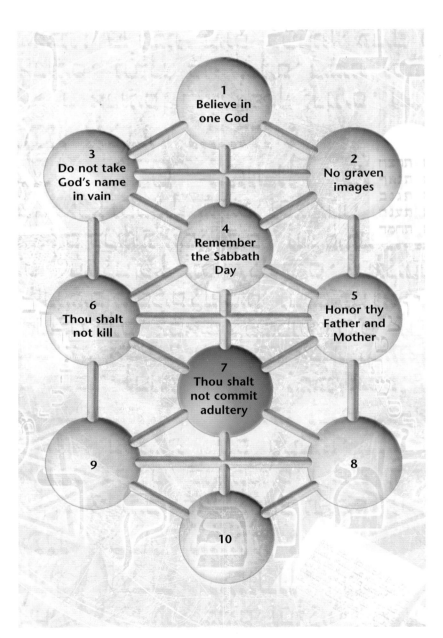

1
Believe in
one God

3
Do not take
God's name
in vain

2
No graven
images

4
Remember
the Sabbath
Day

6
Thou shalt
not kill

5
Honor thy
Father and
Mother

7
Thou shalt
not commit
adultery

9

8

10

This corresponds to Yesod (feeling) of Kadmon. Yesod corresponds to the expression of sexual energies, which is one of the most powerful energies on the planet: poets and mystics have long since recognized that the ecstasy experienced at the height of the sexual act can be likened to spiritual experience.

Studies on our nearest biological relatives, the chimpanzees and pygmy chimps, and more distant cousins, baboons and gorillas, have produced some interesting facts about humans. There are very large differences between the various great ape species when it comes to sexuality and pair bonding: some species, such as the pygmy chimpanzee, are completely promiscuous, with virtually no pair bonding at all; while others, such as the gorilla, will mate more or less for life. *Homo sapiens* seems to appear around the middle of this spectrum: compared with other, similar species we are not very promiscuous, but by no means totally loyal either.

Although we are more than simply animals driven by instincts, these instincts have to be taken into account. From a spiritual viewpoint, the energies released during sex are also spiritual energies. If they are to be harnessed correctly, to help on the journey of return, then they must be channeled correctly. In almost all human societies, this can happen most easily in a stable, one-to-one relationship. But when the biology—both male and female—of our species inclines us not to do this automatically, other social factors must come into play to prohibit such behavior.

Da'ath in Atziluth the Abyss
This is the place of the great Abyss in Atziluth: it is the highest point on the ladder at which an Abyss exists. Above is perfection, below is creation—

Briah, at stage 10. From here, spiritual energy pours down to humanity in stage 10. This stage represents the true archetype of knowledge.

In the Old Testament, when a man "knew" a woman, this was a reference to sexual union. Use of this word is not an accident: knowledge is the attribute of Da'ath, the result of the union of wisdom or Chockmah, the archetypal masculine, and understanding or Binah, the archetypal feminine. When we truly know something, we have united with it—and it has become a part of us, we a part of it.

Kavannah *Intention*

The practice of kavannah was once central to Kabbalist teaching. It has no direct translation into English, but a sense of it can be found in: intention, concentration, devotion, focus, directing something to something else. Whenever kavannah is absent in a meditation or prayer, the gesture is empty.

Devakuth *Cleaving to God*

This spiritual practice is akin to the peak of the mountain for the Kabbalist. Once the techniques of kavannah (knowledge), hitbodedut (meditation), and tzeruf (letter permutations) have become second nature, and the Kabbalist can perform them while eating, walking, and talking, then he or she is ready for devakuth (cleaving to God). This involves withdrawal of thought, of focus, from all the lower worlds. The first withdrawal is from the outer world, from Assiah. The Kabbalist does not stop being active in the world, but his or her focus is withdrawn from it. This is followed by withdrawal from Yetzirah, the world of inner forms and emotions, and then from Briah, the world of thought itself. All that is left is Atziluth, and at this level of consciousness, all there is, is God.

The greatest Kabbalists could maintain devakuth at all times during their waking days. The experience of one Kabbalist was secretly recorded in a diary kept over a fifty-year period. Joseph Caro was a famous lawyer who lived in Safed in Palestine during the Golden Age of Kabbalah, in the mid-16th century. He describes the experience of ecstasy and the encounter with a celestial maggid. Maggid means "one who relates," and usually indicates wandering preachers, but the celestial maggid were archetypal forces who spoke through the Kabbalist's mouth. Caro's maggid called itself "sovereignty"—another title of the sephira Malkuth, the kingdom.

The union of the King, the archetypal masculine, with the Queen, the archetypal feminine. "Union in Alchemy": from Donum Dei, 17th century.

Stage 8 Archetype of Eight

The Eighth Commandment
Thou shalt not steal

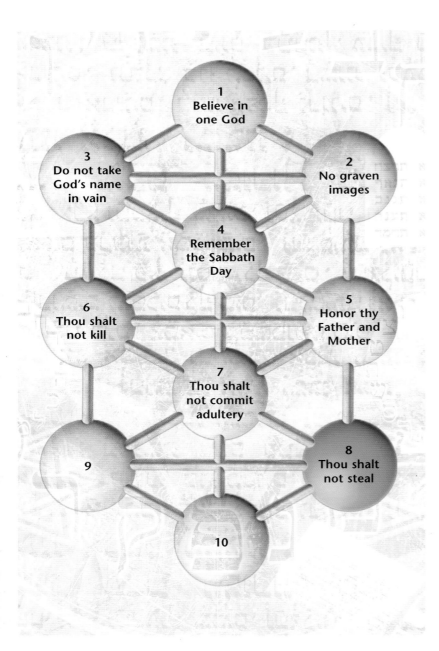

1 Believe in one God

2 No graven images

3 Do not take God's name in vain

4 Remember the Sabbath Day

5 Honor thy Father and Mother

6 Thou shalt not kill

7 Thou shalt not commit adultery

8 Thou shalt not steal

9

10

The eighth commandment represents Netzach of Kadmon. The qualities of Netzach are unselfishness and valor.

Stealing can occur on many different levels. Taking an apple from the display and not putting it in the basket at the checkout; knocking a couple of minutes off the end of a meditation; not pulling your full weight—physically, mentally, or emotionally—in some shared endeavor. All these are a type of stealing. And although at the time it is the group, or the meditation, or the shop that is diminished in some large or small measure, ultimately, the individual who has stolen is the one who is diminished.

The Kabbalist knows that, in any interchange of energies, in any contact between two systems, there will ultimately be a balance: equal amounts of energy will flow both ways. This two-way interaction will not, however, always be a conscious one.

What occurs energetically when something is stolen? Before the act is committed, there is an awareness of equilibrium: an apple is to be paid for at the checkout; a meditation is to last a certain length of time; the shared endeavor requires a specific amount of commitment. These things are known, on a conscious or unconscious level. Then, some other factor, which will have its own rights or wrongs, enters the equation. Hunger means the apple is eaten before the checkout is reached; the telephone goes in the middle of the meditation; a conflict of interests puts pressure on time to be spent on the endeavor. Next comes the decision to keep the imbalance. This decision is also made either consciously or unconsciously: it is only an apple and not worth mentioning at the checkout; answering the telephone is more interesting than finishing the meditation; another task is more important than this endeavor. Lastly comes the reckoning. Energy has been kept back for an ego-centered purpose, rather than being given selflessly and appropriately. There is no balance, so the system starts to move out of equilibrium. The apple gives indigestion because it was eaten too quickly; the telephone call is from an extremely angry person—if the person had called ten minutes later he or she would have been calmer; the shared endeavor fails because there was not quite enough energy behind it.

There is nothing wrong with wanting to have good things. But stealing them from others is not the way to go about getting them.

Chesed of Atziluth *El*

The God of Chesed (mercy) is called El, written Aleph-Lamed. Aleph is the ox, and Lamed is the ox-goad. This gives a good picture of the role of El at this position: from stage 7, the divine force pours across the Abyss. Here that force, characterized by the Aleph, is guided, channeled into forms and focus, characterized by the Lamed.

El could be considered to be a divine Father Christmas. He is the cosmic giver: all the forms of the lower worlds have their origins at this point: we just need to ask, and we shall receive them. The catch? The catch is that nothing in life is free, but stage 8 is the toy shop: we are piling the basket full of goodies, and the checkout is to be found at stage 9!

Prayer

Prayer has always been an important part of Kabbalistic practice. The Way of Prayer is at the core of the teachings of the Baal Shem Tov (the Besht). Before him, much of the Kabbalah was for the spiritual pioneer willing to sacrifice all earthly

pleasure for the greater pleasure of communing with God. For the Besht, it was important to make the teaching more accessible, so that more people could benefit from knowing the Kabbalah. Previously difficult practices were simplified, so that everybody could practice them: devakuth (cleaving to God) became a celebration of the Divine found in everyday life. Kavannah (concentration) was reinterpreted as consciously serving God through good acts.

Until very recently, it was also like this for the gentile Qabalist—special techniques, rituals, and "words of power" placed the Qabalah firmly beyond everyday experience: it was for the occultist who desired hidden powers, and had no relevance to anybody else. Many modern interpreters of Qabalah, by initially expressing Qabalist ideas in a psychological form, have made their relevance clear to everyone.

St. Nicholas, known to all as Santa Claus, shows qualities of giving and unselfishness, the main qualities of Netzach.

Prayer is central to the Kabbalah, in particular to the teachings of the Besht.

Stage 9 Archetype of Nine

The Ninth Commandment
Thou shalt not bear false witness

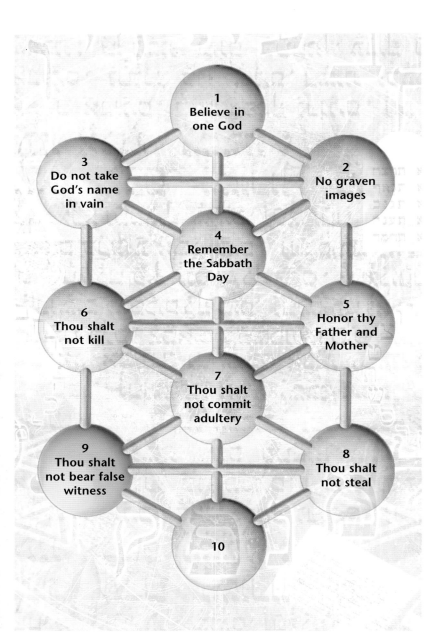

This stage represents Hod of Kadmon, the sephira of communication. The ninth commandment basically means "Do not lie." The story of the boy who cried wolf will be familiar to many.

The boy would come down from the hills, where he tended his flock of sheep, crying that a wolf was attacking his charges. The villagers would run up to where the flock was, only to find there was no wolf, and the boy would laugh that he had tricked them. He did this over and over again. Then, one day, a wolf really did come and start to attack the sheep. The boy ran to the village, but the villagers laughed at him and said, "We're not falling for your tricks this time!" So the boy went back to protect his sheep alone, and the wolf ate him.

Lies can create a momentum of their own: untruth builds upon falsehood, until a person is trapped under a whole construction of lies from which there is no escape. There is always a danger of the entire framework crumbling and crushing that person. It is far better not to start the process.

Lies can result in self-destruction, as in the story of the boy who cried "Wolf!," in which a young shepherd's lies lead to him being eaten by a wolf.

Geburah in Atziluth *Elohim Gebor*

Elohim Gebor means "God of Battles." The early
Semites actually had a Warrior Goddess, so maybe
the God-name of this stage should be "Eloh
Geborah." The tradition of warrior goddesses is not
an uncommon one in pastoral societies. There is also
a link with the devouring mother goddesses, such as
the Hindu goddess Kali, who kill their children
without mercy, but only when it is necessary—the
killing is never gratuitous. It will come from a
requirement to balance out an imbalance: it is not
"bad" as such, simply devoid of mercy (Chesed).

Shamanic Gods

The action of Eloh Geborah is clearly seen through
the teachings of the shamans of Central and South
America. The shamanistic view is one of the
conservation of spiritual energy. The gods give
spiritual energy to humans so that they may create in
Assiah. Humans receive the energy and transform it
into whatever they are creating. This creation is not
necessarily physical: it can be anything from a
beautiful handmade tapestry to a poem, a music
album, or a mass-produced car.

The important thing about it is that through the
gift of the gods, the ingenuity and creative forces of
humankind have brought something new into the
universe. The shaman believes that this is an
extremely important function: humanity is unique in
having consciousness right through from Atziluth
(the spiritual world) to Assiah (the physical world).

Humanity's ability to "solidify the spirit" is
deeply profound: by doing this, the energy is actually
multiplied many times. Only a small amount of the
creation then needs to be returned to the gods for the
cosmic accounts to balance. This balancing is done,
according to the shaman, by making an offering to

the gods of some of the produce. This concept is
behind the "tithe," a tax taking the form of a
donation of a tenth of an individual's produce to his
or her synagogue or church. Although very few
people create tangible products these days, some still
give a percentage of their income.

But what happens when creation
occurs on a massive scale—at a level
incomprehensible before now?
According to the shaman, as humanity
has lost consciousness of the gods and
conscious sacrifice, so it happens
unconsciously instead. Concern for
superficial attributes has diverted our
minds from the spiritual path. This
imbalance has led to a lack of humanity,
sometimes resulting in the most dire
consequences. On a spiritual level, by
losing touch with God, humanity has
reverted to blood sacrifice.

*The shaman teaches us that
humans alone are given God's
energy to let us create. If we
forget this, God exacts
a price.* Medicine Mask
Dance *by P. Kane (1810–71).*

*Kali, the Hindu mother goddess,
murders and eats her children in
order to balance out an imbalance.*

Stage 10 Archetype of Ten

The Tenth Commandment *Thou shalt not covet thy neighbor's belongings*

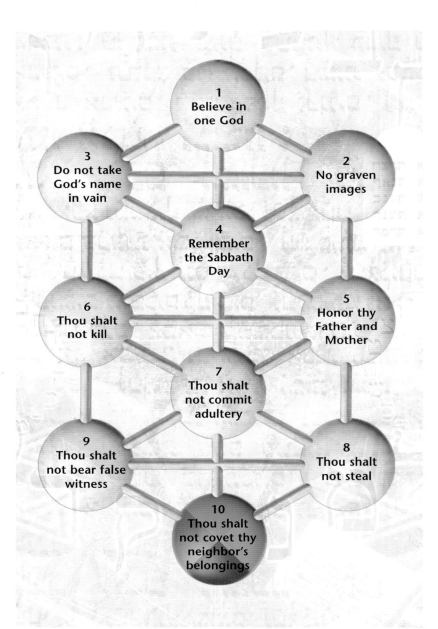

1
Believe in
one God

3
Do not take
God's name
in vain

2
No graven
images

4
Remember
the Sabbath
Day

6
Thou shalt
not kill

5
Honor thy
Father and
Mother

7
Thou shalt
not commit
adultery

9
Thou shalt
not bear false
witness

8
Thou shalt
not steal

10
Thou shalt
not covet thy
neighbor's
belongings

This commandment is associated with Malkuth of Kadmon. To covet is to yearn for, long for, crave, hanker after, and desire. In the original text, the belongings mentioned are house, wife, slave, ox or ass, or anything else owned by a neighbor. If the commandments had been written today, the list would almost certainly also cover job, lifestyle and bank balance. But why would doing this be a sin—after all, coveting in itself does not physically harm anyone?

The obvious answer, of course, is that there is often only a small step between coveting something and going out and taking it: history is littered with countless wars that have started in just this way. But stealing is dealt with in the eighth commandment: there is something more subtle happening here.

The tenth stage is the place of the ultimate spark of humanity at the core of every one of us. Each spark is unique, and we all have our own destiny to unfold, in our own time and in our own way. By saying, even just to ourselves, "I prefer what that person has to what I have," we are at this level denying our own individuality, denying that the situation we have created for ourselves right here and now is absolutely perfect, and fulfills all that we require.

This is the last stage of the journey. Here in Malkuth is where Adam Kadmon stands, and where the essential spark of humanity exists. This is where Man meets God, and the journey of return ultimately ends. Stage 10 is the next step, the final frontier.

Tiphareth in Atziluth *Eloah va Da'ath*

This God-name means "the Omniscient One"—the all-knower, at the center of everything. In Christian Cabala, this stage is represented by the light of the

East Window, streaming through from God beyond. In the architecture of many sacred buildings, when the form of the ladder is plotted onto the physical layout, this is the point of the high altar: indeed, in ancient temples and churches, the building physically stops at this point, with the altar hard up against the east wall.

This is also the place of the Holy Grail, which rests on the high altar. In Arthurian myth, the quest for the Grail was the task set for only the very best of the Knights of the Round Table.

The quest represents the search for the very highest within us all. Only the purest of spirit, the most selfless of knights, were able to succeed in this quest. This is what is achieved when this stage is fully realized.

Kether of Briah   *Metatron*

The archangel of Kether (crown) is Metatron. Traditionally, Metatron is the patriarch Enoch—he who "walked with God and was not." Once a human consciousness passes into the level of the archetypal, it cannot stay human—it cannot stay in a physical body. Hence Enoch "was not" when he achieved this stage of consciousness.

This is the place in us that knows. It is the space beyond the stillness inside. At this point all creation begins. This is where our individual sparks arise. This is the core of who we are, which remains constant throughout all experience. A belief in reincarnation would see this as the point to which all the experiences of all our different lives return: it is the highest point of conscious experience.

Here, all teachings are one, all knowledge the same knowledge. It becomes clear at this stage of consciousness that the teachings of the world—Kabbalah, Christianity, Islam, the Mystery schools, Hinduism, Buddhism, Shamanism—are all the same teaching.

Light pouring through church windows represents the light of God.

Sir Galahad, one of the most virtuous knights of the Round Table, who strove to regain the Holy Grail.

CHAPTER 8

Kabbalistic Speculations

The mysteries of Kabbalah are linked to other areas of modern-day thought—in particular, to psychology, sacred architecture, and the practices of tarot and astrology. This chapter examines the relationship of these disciplines to Kabbalah, beginning with psychology.

Psychology and psychotherapy today seem to hold all the answers as modern-day dispensers of insight into personal and family affairs. How could it be that what describes itself as a science can replace, seemingly so completely, the traditional function of the rabbi, priest, and pastor in force for thousands of years? Have people changed so much that they no longer need the spiritual?

By looking at what psychologists and psychotherapists do, the answer, to this question, most of the time, seems to be "No." These professionals do take on the role once filled by spiritual advisors, but only by dispensing similar wisdom and understanding. There is, of course, a big difference of emphasis, in that there is a recognized distinction between the psyche and the spirit. In fact, dealing with the psyche directly is part of the function once carried out by the great teachers of Kabbalah, as well as the Greek Mystery schools. So psychology could be considered a descendant of

Kabbalah, and has rediscovered a great deal in a relatively short period of time. Indeed, some of the founding fathers of the psychological movement may have been influenced by Kabbalah, as we shall see.

Sigmund Freud

The father of psychotherapy, Sigmund Freud, came from a Jewish family; however, they were not religious, and Freud described himself as an atheist. Having said this, he was familiar with the Kabbalah—his library contained several books on the subject. There are clear indications that parts of his work were similar to the teachings of the 13th-century Spanish Kabbalist, Rabbi Abraham Abulafia.

One of the unusual things about Abulafia's work is that he hid very little behind veils of allusion, but wrote clearly and forthrightly about his spiritual practice. This was extremely unusual: people generally hid what they were doing because they were scared of being discovered. Abulafia seems to have had very little of that particular emotion—at one stage in his life he even attempted to convert the Pope, and survived to tell the tale! In his writings he describes his technique as "jumping and skipping." This is very close to Freud's core technique of "free association," in which the patient is led to reveal deeper layers of his or her own unconscious motivations. Whether Freud was aware of Abulafia or not, the fact is that these techniques were in use 700 years before Freud used them.

Carl Gustav Jung

C. G. Jung studied with Freud. He had a life-long interest in alchemy, and he wrote extensively on the subject. For him, alchemy was a metaphor for an inner experience which he called "individuation." This is an inner drive that moves each of us to greater wholeness and integration of mind, body, and spirit. Kabbalistically, this call is the urge to "Return to the Garden." For Jung, the inner world was just as real as the outer world was. He coined the term "psyche," meaning the entire being, not just the conscious mind.

Roberto Assagioli

Assagioli was a contemporary of Jung, and like him studied with Freud in Vienna. He was an Italian Jew with a deep interest in the Kabbalah, although he never publicized this. He also worked with

Abraham Maslow in the 1960s to create a humanistic psychology, which focuses on the mentally well human being, rather than on the mentally ill. His contribution to humanistic psychology is psychosynthesis. His egg diagram (see overleaf), which is central to his work, can be related to the Tree of Life quite easily (see page 20).

Sigmund Freud (1856–1939) was familiar with the doctrines of Kabbalah. His work, particularly his technique of "free association," shows traces of its influence.

Carl Jung (1875–1961) developed a theory of "individuation" that can be related to the Kabbalah and the "Return to the Garden."

Psychology Spiritual Growth

There were several significant differences between C.G. Jung and his teacher, Sigmund Freud. One difference was their understanding of the unconscious. Another was the question of what motivated people.

Perception, imagination, reason, and insight lead us up the ladder toward an understanding of the divine word. Beyond that is God—who cannot be understood. R. Fludd, Utriusque Cosmi, Vol. 2, Oppenheim, 1619.

Freud viewed unconscious content as being derived entirely from lost or repressed childhood memories. Human motivation, he felt, could be understood by the interplay of two basic drives: self-preservation and the pleasure principle, which he called "libido." Both were essentially conscious processes.

Jung, working with both well and unwell people in his practice, consistently found the same images arising in his patients' drawings and paintings, and as recurring themes in their dreams. These images would usually have no meaning to the conscious minds of his patients, yet he recognized them as symbols used in the Mystery teachings in both the East and the West. They were symbols of wholeness, of completeness and integration: four-foldness, mandalas (unbroken circles), and wise, kind teachers were common.

Jung felt that although self-preservation and the libido were contained in the unconscious mind, it also included far more. He felt that the drive to improve, to change, to become a well-adjusted, balanced personality was often to be found in the unconscious rather than the conscious mind. Individuation, the process of striving toward wholeness (see page 110), became central to his work, and is essentially the process of climbing the Ladder of Light.

Avoiding Spiritual Growth

Treading the path of return is a scary business. The fear comes from the "little I," the ego, for whom it represents the threat of annihilation. It comes as no surprise, then, that the ego will often try to undermine the individual's spiritual growth, either by rejecting it, or by side-tracking it to make it harmless. Assagioli identified seven different ways in which this resistance can occur, which are very well described in the book *What We May Be*, written by one of his foremost students, Piero Ferrucci.

The Seven Ways of Resistance

Binah The ego attempts to avoid spiritual growth by repressing all memories and thoughts of the spiritual. This leads to the typical Binah/Saturnine feelings of isolation, deep melancholy, and an indefinable sense of loss.

Chesed Here the ego turns spiritual experience into something harmless by making it routine. Direct, real experience is replaced by slogans and rituals that are full of glamor, but empty of meaning.

Organized religion can demonstrate this, as can any teaching focused on a single, powerful personality such as a spiritual leader or guru.

Geburah Another way to lose true contact with the spiritual is to dogmatize the experience. This is the experience of musts and oughts: "I must eat brown rice twice a day if I want to go to heaven," "I should be joyful." This brings an excess of judgement into our lives and not enough mercy.

Tiphareth Defensive pessimism is another all-too-common avoidance strategy: the individual feels that, for one reason or another, they will make no further progress: "I am too old," "My work does not leave me enough time to meditate." These thoughts are accompanied by feelings of self-pity and impotence.

Netzach The ego can react to spiritual growth by compensating with the opposite feeling: for example, after a powerful love experience, a person can become inexplicably hateful. Any creative impulse can be followed by the desire to destroy it.

Hod One particularly powerful defense against a spiritual experience is "desacralization." The ego attacks the experience by ridiculing it, or trying to analyze it and belittle it. This cynical exercise aims to redefine the sacred in intellectual terms—which of course it cannot hope to do.

Yesod The ego can use projection to good effect. The individual can accept the reality of spiritual experience, but put the responsibility for the experience onto a guru or teacher. This means that the spiritual can be held at arm's length, and is no longer in a position to threaten the ego.

ASSAGIOLI'S EGG DIAGRAM

The egg, representing an individual, is the complete tree. The lower section—the lower unconscious—is the sephira Malkuth (body), and the world of Assiah (the physical world). The central band, the middle unconscious, is the sephiroth Yesod (feeling) up to Chesed (mercy), and the world of Yetzirah. The circle in the center of the central band, the field of awareness, is the sephira Tiphareth (balance). The higher section of the egg, representing the higher unconscious or "superconscious," is the supernal triangle above the Abyss, and the world of Briah (the mental world). The top of the egg, the place of the transpersonal, or spiritual self, is the sephira Kether (crown), and the World of Atziluth (the spiritual world).

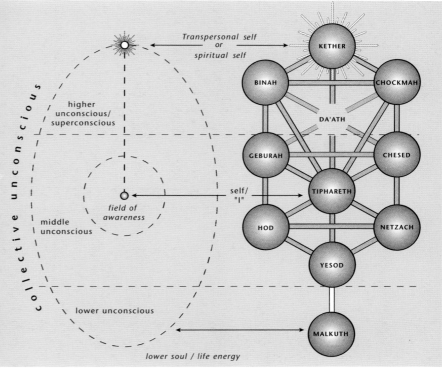

Psychology the Nature of Evil

In the past, the source of all evil was considered to be the Devil: an external, objective entity that could be understood quite simply and guarded against. Anything that went wrong in a person's life could be put down to "the Devil and all his works." Nowadays, with belief in God less common than it was, and belief in the Devil even rarer, the source of evil is far more difficult to define.

In the Garden of Eden, the Devil took physical form and worked to thwart God's will by tempting Eve. His function now is to help us on the return to Paradise.

There were two views on evil: it was either objective or subjective:

Objective evil

A force "out there" in the world that an individual rejects by consciously fighting against it, or accepts—either actively or passively. A person is not necessarily wholly evil, although wholly evil people do exist.

Subjective evil

This is one individual or group's judgement that the actions of another individual or group are "evil." People who do evil things—rapists, child molesters, serial killers—are psychologically damaged through experiences, often in childhood, which have caused a normal, balanced person to become unbalanced.

In the Kabbalah, the emphasis is on balance: any excess toward the left or right pillar should be brought back to the center. Evil comes in an excess of one quality: any quality of the sephiroth, taken to extremes, can become evil. The expansive principle of Chesed, good in a growing child, can lead to cancer when excessive in an adult's body cells. An excess of the passion of Netzach can lead to obsessional behavior. But this tells only part of the story.

The Devil

The Christian concepts of evil and the Devil have their roots in the Bible. There are two different views of the Devil in the Old Testament. In Genesis, as the serpent in the garden, he is the tempter that persuades Eve to eat of the fruit of the Tree of Knowledge of good and evil: here he is represented as working against the will of God.

In the Book of Job, he is Job's tormentor, but working very specifically under God's direction: "all that he (Job) has is in your hand, but do not harm his person."

Judaic legend has it that the archangel Michael had a twin, called Sammael. When God created humankind, Sammael believed it was a great mistake, and was cast out of Heaven. He took on the new name of Lucifer or Satan, and is now "down here" to torment us. But Michael still guards us from the worst of his brother's attentions.

In one version of Kabbalistic lore, Lucifer and humankind are intimately linked. Both underwent a fall: humankind from paradise, the world of Briah, and Satan from heaven, the world of Atziluth. We are both now on the path of return, climbing back up to our former positions.

The "great deceiver" has a very specific role in humankind's journey: he must help us to remember why we are here. In turn, he will not be allowed his own return until he has assisted us in ours.

The Abyss and the Klippoth

Another Kabbalistic tradition speaks of a "shadow tree"—the Tree of the Klippoth. The word *klippoth* means husk or empty shell. Some ancient tales speak of earlier creations than this current one, each of which fell out of the perfect consciousness of

Adam Kadmon and into the Abyss: they were mistakes, and had been abandoned. They lay here still, shells of experience lurking in the shadow of the ladder beneath the Briatic Abyss. These "tunnels" have their own sets of symbols, of demons and dark princes, just as the tree has its angels and archangels.

This idea was not much favored by the pious Jews, who found it hard to accept the idea that God could make mistakes, so this particular story was destined to become a part of the oral Kabbalistic tradition.

However, the idea was accepted and developed by the Christian Cabalists, who felt that identifying exactly who the enemy was would assist their spiritual development. This idea became the basis for the large number of stories about Faustus, such as Goethe's *Faust*, who called up and made a pact with the Devil.

Satan tormented Job but worked in accordance with God's wishes.

Dr. Faustus, a popular character in fiction, sold his soul to the Devil.

The Ladder of Light in Architecture

In studying the architecture of the ancient and medieval world, it is impossible to know exactly how much of a coincidence it is that the ground plan of a temple or cathedral matches with the diagram known today as the Ladder of Light. The plans and correspondences are presented here, to let the reader be their own judge.

Masons and Templars

The stonemasons who were involved in building the churches and cathedrals of Western Europe in the 11th to 14th centuries had a great deal of knowledge of or access to some form of esoteric teaching: this is shown by the fact that symbols and figures carved on the stones of these buildings use consistently an unusual, non-Christian imagery. Was the source of these images the masons themselves, or the "hierarchy" that directed their work?

The inspiration for such carvings has been the subject of specumuch lation. The crusades came to an end during this time. Many who returned from the Holy Land and threw themselves into the construction of the cathedrals brought back more than just their weapons and belongings. They

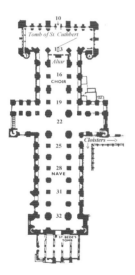

Top: Glastonbury Abbey plan (c. 1585 CE).

Above: Durham Cathedral plan.

Right: Men at work on a 15th-century building site.

brought to Europe a myriad of Greek, Arabic, and Hebrew ideas and documents, which were to lay the foundations of the Renaissance, just a few generations later.

The Knights Templar

One organization that has often been cited as a source of this type of mystical influence is the Order of Poor Knights of the Temple of Solomon—also known as the Knights Templar. From humble beginnings they became an extremely rich and highly influential order, until their overthrow in the early 14th century. They commissioned many unusual churches and other buildings.

There were many stories about the Templars: that they worshiped a god called Baphomat, and reviled the Christian God. Exactly what mysteries they knew will probably never be discovered, but there has been speculation that, when the founders of the order were based in Jerusalem during the first crusade, they found some teaching, knowledge, or treasure that enabled them to accumulate great wealth.

When the Templars were disbanded by papal decree between 1307 and 1314, many of the order fled to Scotland—one of the few places in the Christian world where they knew they would be welcomed. Scotland was then at war with the English and needed fighting men, and the Pope had recently excommunicated Robert the Bruce, so the Templars knew that the decree would not be enforced there.

Whatever the truth about the Templars, they have left behind an extraordinary legacy of churches. One such is Rossyln chapel, just south of Edinburgh in Scotland. Seemingly a simple parish church on the outside, the inside is covered with exquisite carvings of green men, stars, and sigils—

The Knights Templar were instrumental in the building of many churches and other buildings before their overthrow in the early 14th century.

and, most impressive of all, two pillars to the left and right of the altar, known as the Master and the Apprentice pillars. This chapel was commissioned by Lord St. Clair of Orkney, and is full of Templar symbolism, and the Saint Clairs were also the hereditary heads of the Scottish freemasons.

Freemasonry

This is a semisecret society that thrives to this day. Masons trace their ancestry back to Hiram, the architect of the Temple of Jerusalem. However, "speculative" masonry—that is to say, freemasonry for non-Craftsmen—officially started in 1717, with the foundation of the first Grand Lodge in London, England. Historic links to the "Craft" masonry of the cathedral builders have been established.

Many Scottish masons were active in France in the 17th century, and were closely linked to the Jacobite rebellion of "Bonnie Prince Charlie"— the Scottish Rite today plays a central part in Masonic meetings.

Other early Speculative Masons were linked to important events of the Enlightenment and key figures in the French Revolution and the American Declaration of Independence were freeemasons.

Tarot and the Mystery Teachings

Historically, the existence of tarot is first recorded in the 14th century, and although none of the packs mentioned in the documents of the day have survived, the chances are that they were in circulation for a long time before they were written about. Whatever their exact origins, there is little doubt that the pictures represent the teachings of a Mystery school, disguised as a game of cards so that they would not attract unwanted attention.

Hiding evidence of the Mysteries was a common practice in medieval times, when the price for openly studying them was excommunication or death. One way of hiding teachings was in stories. About the same time as tarot may have appeared, the stories of King Arthur and his Knights of the Round Table and their quest for the Holy Grail emerged onto the European scene.

These stories have themes common to many cultures. At least one contemporary Western Mystery School uses Round Table and Grail castle imagery as a central part of its teachings of the Qabalah.

The origins of tarot are uncertain, and its early forms vary. One school of thought states that they preserve in pictorial form the teachings of the Egyptian priests of Anubis.

Tarot cards became popular in the 15th century among the aristocracy of Renaissance Italy, with especially beautiful packs being made for the Medici and other influential families.

Many early tarot packs that are mentioned in contemporary documents have not survived to the present day. One pack that has is the Tarocchi of Mantegna (see below). Another group of packs that

The Wheel of Fortune tarot card from the Visconti Sforza deck.

SYMBOLISM IN THE CARDS

One of the earliest tarot packs, the "Tarocchi" of Mantegna, appeared in the 15th century. It is thought to have been made by Parrasio Michele, Master of the School of Ferrara. There is no doubt that the influence of Hermetic/Kabbalistic thought can be seen in their design. This pack consists of five suits of ten cards each, and the correspondences to the five worlds of the Ladder of Light are shown opposite.

The Strength card from the Tarot of Mantegna.

are still extant were commissioned by the Visconti-Sforza families, after whom they are named. These packs consist of four suits and twenty-two trumps. Each suit is made up of cards numbered one to ten, and four "court cards." This is exactly the form that contemporary tarot packs take.

The minor cards one to ten correspond to the ten sephiroth of the Tree of Life, from Kether to Malkuth. The suits and the court cards correspond to the elements and worlds, as shown below.

Suit	Court card	Element	World
Coins	King	Earth	Assiah
Cups	Queen	Water	Yetzirah
Swords	Page	Air	Briah
Staffs	Knight	Fire	Atziluth

Court de Gebelin and the Egyptian connection

In 1781 a Parisian freemason by the name of Antoine Court de Gebelin published a nine-volume work called *The Primitive World*. In it, he states that tarot originated in Egypt and was brought to Europe by the gypsies, whose origins were also said to be in Egypt. In the late 18th century, reading tarot cards was seen as a parlor game. However, this thesis created a revitalized interest in them. Within only a few years, the salons of Paris were filled with people who considered having their tarot cards read de rigueur.

Tarot and Qabalah

The first person to map the tarot trumps to the Tree of Life was the French Qabalist Eliphas Levi in the 19th century. His version put the Magician—trump 1—on the 13th path and ended with the Fool—trump 0—on the 32nd path.

This sequence of tarot/Tree of Life correspondences was reinterpreted by the Golden Dawn. S. L. McGregor Mathers moved the Fool to the start of the sequence, at path 13, so that the last card was the World—trump 21.

Mathers also swapped the cards Strength and Justice, because this fitted the mapping of the cards onto the tree. These two were swapped back by Aleister Crowley in his Thoth Tarot pack, but almost all the tarot packs published since the 1930s have used the Golden Dawn attributions.

The Justice (Adjustment) tarot card from the Thoth deck by Aleister Crowley and Dame Frieda Harris.

CORRESPONDENCES IN THE TAROCCHI OF MANTEGNA

Suit	Images	World
Humanity	The outer world of humanity: social forms	Assiah
Muses	The inner world of humanity, artistic creation	Yetzirah
Liberal Arts	The powers of human thought	Briah
Cardinal Virtues	The conscience: spiritual development and refinement of the soul	Atziluth
Cosmic Spheres	Cosmic order expressed in all facets of the universe	Adam Kadmon

This form of tarot has not survived through to the present day.

Astrology: Kabbalah and the Planets

Astrology has a history at least as long as Kabbalah, and there have always been symbolic links between them. At the beginning of the last century, the founders of the society of the Golden Dawn drew up the correspondences that are usually used today.

These link various astrological symbols to the 22 paths of the Tree of Life, also to the 22 tarot trumps, and the 22 letters of the Hebrew alphabet. The Hebrew letters, which divide up into three groups, link the three mother letters to the elements air, water, and fire; the seven double letters to the seven classical planets; and the twelve single letters to the twelve signs of the zodiac. (See Correspondences in the Appendix, pages 124–125.)

The Seven Classical Planets

Until recently only seven "planets" were known in classical astronomy/astrology (the distinction between the two was only drawn in the 18th century). The term referred to moving lights in the sky—which included the sun and the moon. It was not until 1785 that a planet outside of Saturn's orbit, Uranus, was discovered. Two more planets—Neptune and Pluto—have been discovered since, plus innumerable asteroids and a few planetoids, the best known of these being Chiron.

Saturn As the most distant of the classical planets, Saturn represented the outer limits, time, and old age. Its color is black. It corresponds generally to the Abyss and supernal sephiroth, in that these are unknown and unseen from below. Specifically, Saturn corresponds to the third sephira, Binah, the Great Mother.

Jupiter Also known as the "Great Benefic," Jupiter is a very positive influence in the astrological birth chart. It relates well to the qualities of the fourth sephira, Chesed (mercy). Its color is royal blue.

Mars Mars' color is red. In the birth chart, it indicates where an individual moves out into their world. It corresponds to the fifth sephira, Geburah (severity).

Sun Just as Tiphareth (balance) is at the center of the Tree of Life, and astronomically the sun is at the center of the solar system, so astrologically it represents the core of our being in this life. Its color is golden yellow.

Venus The planet of love, talents, and beauty, Venus corresponds with the seventh sephira, Netzach (passion). The color of both is green, corresponding to the green Orphic teaching ray.

Mercury In the birth-chart, Mercury represents communications and travel, which ties in with the qualities of the eighth sephira, Hod (thought). The color of both is orange, corresponding to the orange Hermetic teaching ray.

Moon The moon is the planet of tides, rhythmic change, and the unconscious mind, paralleling the qualities of Yesod (feeling), the ninth sephira.

The New Planets

Astrologically, the new planets have come to represent all the vast changes of the last four to five centuries. Kabbalah has also taken on some of these planets, but the attributions are less certain.

Uranus Discovered in 1784, at the dawn of the Industrial Revolution, this planet has come to be associated with sudden upheavals and unforeseen events. It is linked in astrology with the sign of Aquarius. Kabbalistically, the association is with Chockmah (wisdom), whose power, if experienced directly, is equally revolutionary.

Neptune Discovered in 1830, at the dawn of a revolution in thinking, Neptune has come to be associated with the power behind revolution and mass movements, often unseen but immensely influential in the end—both Marx and Darwin were writing and influencing people at this time. Some associate this planet with Kether (crown).

Pluto Discovered by accident in 1930, just as the nuclear age dawned and humans discovered that they had the power to destroy the earth, this planet is linked to powers of mass destruction and transformation. Astrologically, these dark powers have linked the planet with Scorpio. Kabbalistically, the strongest association is with Da'ath (knowledge).

Earth This was not properly discovered as a planet until the 1960s, when the Apollo missions began to send back pictures of Earth from space. Earth is still rarely used in the birth chart as a separate planet, although the position on the planet relative to the sun is a fundamental measurement. The 1960s were a time of a mass change in consciousness, the ramifications of which have still to unfold fully, but two important movements that were birthed at this time are feminism and ecology. Both link the planet to the sephira Malkuth (body).

The main links between Kabbalah and astrology are shown in the correspondences between the planets and the paths of the Tree of Life.

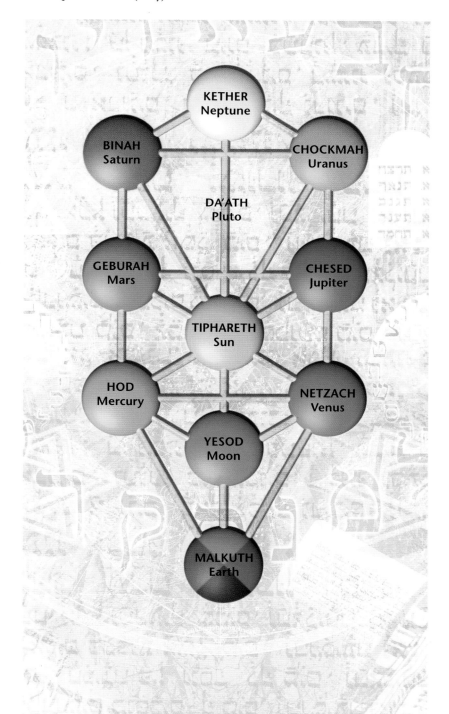

Astrology: Kabbalah and the Signs

Linking up a system of twelve signs going around in a circle, with the ten sephiroth of the Tree of Life cannot give a straightforward one-to-one match! However, there are some close ties between the two systems, and the following list indicates some of them.

The "Houses"

In an astrological chart, there are twelve "houses," starting with the first house at the point of the eastern horizon, or "Ascendant," and continuing counterclockwise around the entire circle of the chart, so that the twelfth house ends where the first begins. These twelve houses have a very similar meaning to the twelve signs of the Zodiac, so they are considered together in the comparisons below.

Zodiac Man (from the 14th or 15th century) relates the human body to the signs of the Zodiac.

Rulerships

Each sign and house is strongly associated with a certain planet. In the classical astrological system, each of the five planets rules two signs each, and the sun and moon one each. In modern-day astrology, the new outer planets—Uranus, Neptune, and Pluto—have also been given "co-rulerships" of signs.

1 Aries The first sign of spring is Aries (the Ram); the first house on the birthchart is the point of sunrise—they both represent new beginnings, as well as being right at the end of the old cycle. The first house also represents the self in a birth chart. All these things have connotations of the Kether–Tiphareth–Malkuth relationship, in which the Tiphareth of one tree is both the Kether of the tree below as well as the Malkuth of the tree above.

2 Taurus The planet Venus rules the sign of Taurus (the Bull) and the second house. They are all linked to sensual, beautiful things, and therefore to the sephiroth of Netzach.

3 Gemini The sephira Hod is associated with the mercurial Gemini (the Twins) and the third house: how they are placed in a birth chart indicate how a person communicates with the world.

4 Cancer The Crab, the animal associated with the sign of Cancer, lives in the sea and on the seashore, areas strongly influenced by the moon. Cancer and the fourth house represent the mother, the unconscious mind, and hidden beginnings—the nine-month gestation period before the birth of spring at Aries. All these things link them to the sephira Yesod, the foundation.

5 Leo Linked with self-expression and creativity, Leo (the Lion) and the fifth house have strong associations with the sephira Netzach—even though they are both ruled by the sun.

6 Virgo Ruled by Mercury, Virgo (the Virgin) and the sixth house are associated with detailed, meticulous work and a sense of order— qualities that relate to the sephira Hod.

7 Libra Libra (the Scales) and the seventh house relate to partners, friends, and enemies. Kabbalistic astrology sees this as the place of Tiphareth, in its aspect of the higher self. The seventh house is opposite the first, the house of the ego. It acts like a mirror, reflecting back the parts of ourselves that we find hard to accept. Others bring those parts back to us.

8 Scorpio Mars rules this sign and house, although in modern-day astrology Pluto also co-rules them. The eighth house is the house of sex and death, and also inheritances. Scorpio (the Scorpion) has a strong drive to self-transformation and an uncompromising quality that is strongly reminiscent of the sephira Geburah.

9 Sagittarius The ninth house and Sagittarius (the Centaur), ruled by Jupiter, in a birth chart indicate religion, wealth, travel, and any other qualities that expand an individual's consciousness. They are therefore well matched with the sephira Chesed.

10 Capricorn Saturn rules Capricorn (the Goat) and the tenth house. In a natal chart they indicate a person's relationship to their profession, to authority, and to how they deal with externally imposed limitations. These qualities link them to the sephira Binah.

11 Aquarius The eleventh house is about aspirations and long-term goals; Aquarius (the Water-bearer) is about new horizons. Modern astrology gives the rulership of Aquarius to Uranus, rather than its classical ruler, Saturn. This association therefore links Aquarius and the eleventh house to Chockmah.

12 Pisces Jupiter rules Pisces (the two Fish) and the twelfth house, although modern astrology gives Neptune as a co-ruler. The qualities here are contemplation, retreat, and hidden depths. These associate Pisces with Kether.

The main links between Kabbalah and the Zodiac are shown in the correspondences between the signs and the paths of the Tree of Life.

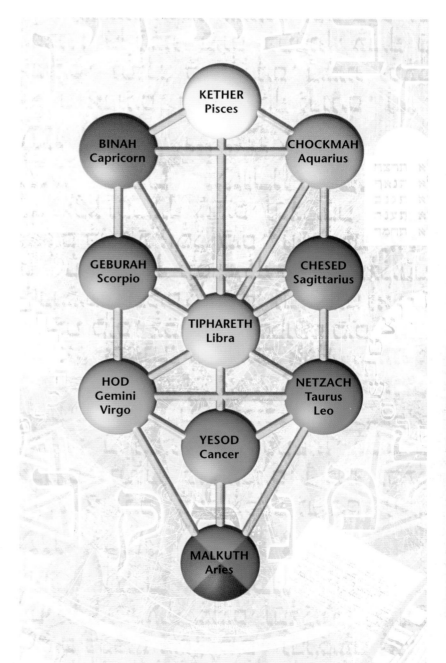

Appendix
Correspondences

	Ladder	Tree	Hebrew
1	Kether in Kadmon, Ain	Kether	1
2	Chockmah in Kadmon, Ain Soph	Chockmah	2
3	Binah in Kadmon, Ain Soph Aur	Binah	3
4	Chesed in Kadmon, Kether in Atziluth	Chesed	4
5	Geburah in Kadmon, Chockmah in Atziluth	Geburah	5
6	Tiphareth in Kadmon, Binah in Atziluth	Tiphareth	6
7	Netzach in Kadmon, Da'ath in Atziluth	Netzach	7
8	Hod in Kadmon, Chesed in Atziluth	Hod	8
9	Yesod in Kadmon, Geburah in Atziluth	Yesod	9
10	Malkuth in Kadmon, Tiphareth in Atziluth, Kether in Briah	Malkuth	10
11	Netzach in Atziluth, Chockmah in Briah	1, 2	Aleph
12	Hod in Atziluth, Binah in Briah	1, 3	Beth
13	Yesod in Atziluth, Da'ath in Briah	1, 6	Gimel
14	Chesed in Briah	2, 3	Daleth
15	Geburah in Briah	2, 6	Heh
16	Malkuth in Atziluth, Tiphareth in Briah, Kether in Yetzirah	2, 4	Vau
17	Netzach in Briah, Chockmah in Yetzirah	3, 6	Zayin
18	Hod in Briah, Binah in Yetzirah	3, 5	Chet
19	Yesod in Briah, Da'ath in Yetzirah	4, 5	Tet
20	Chesed in Yetzirah	4, 6	Yod
21	Geburah in Yetzirah	4, 7	Kaph
22	Malkuth in Briah, Tiphareth in Yetzirah, Kether in Assiah	5, 6	Lamed
23	Netzach in Yetzirah, Chockmah in Assiah	5, 8	Mem
24	Hod in Yetzirah, Binah in Assiah	6, 7	Nun
25	Yesod in Yetzirah, Da'ath in Assiah	6, 9	Samech
26	Chesed in Assiah	6, 8	Ayin
27	Geburah in Assiah	7, 8	Peh
28	Tiphareth in Assiah, Malkuth in Yetzirah	7, 9	Tzadik
29	Netzach in Assiah	7, 10	Qoph
30	Hod in Assiah	8, 9	Resh
31	Yesod in Assiah	8, 10	Shin
32	Malkuth in Assiah	9, 10	Tau

Archetype/Tarot	God/Planet	Archangel	Angels
Crown			
Wisdom			
Understanding			
Mercy	Eheieh		
Severity	IHVH		
Beauty	IHVH Elohim		
Eternity	No attribution		
Reverberation	El		
Foundation	Elohim Gebor		
Kingdom	IHVH Aloah	Metatron	
Fool	IHVH Tzabaoth	Ratziel	
Magician	Elohim Tzabaoth	Tzaphkiel	
High Priestess	Shaddai el Chai	No attribution	
Empress		Tzadkiel	
Emperor		Khamael	
Heirophant	Adonai Ha Aretz	Raphael	Chaioth ha Qadesh: Holy Living Creatures
Lovers		Haniel	Auphanim: Wheels
Chariot		Michael	Aralim: Thrones
Strength		Gabriel	Serpents
Hermit			Chasmalim; Brilliant Ones
Wheel of Fortune			Seraphim; Fiery serpents
Justice	No attribution. Neptune or Sirius	Sandalphon	Malakim: the Kings
Hanged Man	Fixed Stars, Uranus		Elohim: the Gods
Death	Saturn		Beni Elohim: Sons of God
Temperance	Pluto (Chiron)		Kerubim: the Strong
Devil	Jupiter		
Tower	Mars		
Star	Sun		Ashim: Souls of Fire
Moon	Venus		
Sun	Mercury		
Judgement	Moon		
World	Earth		

Bibliography

Kabbalah on the Web

Name	URL	Description
The Hermetic Library	www.hermetic.com	Tarot and the spiritual arts
Colin's Kabbalah Links	www.digital-brilliance.com/kab/nok/index.htm	Excellent place to start research on all types of Kabbalah
Chabad in Cyberspace	www.chabad.org/about.html	Web site of the Chabad-Lubavitch movement
The Inner Dimension	www.inner.org/channel/basics.htm	Basics in Kabbalah and Chassudit
The Kabbalah	www.kheper.auz.com/topics/Kabbalah/index.htm	Kabbalah within the Judaic Tradition
The Kabbalah Society	www.kabbalahsociety.org	Kabbalah in the tradition of the School of Toledo
The Keys to Kabbalah	www.soft.net.uk/ambain/webdoc2.htm	Privately published discourse on the Ladder of Light
"The Ladder of Light"	www.LadderOfLight.com	For further information on the Ladder of Light and the Tree of Life

Published Books

Astrology

Halevi, Warren Kenton *Astrology: the Celestial Mirror,* Thames & Hudson, 1974

Cabala

Bain, Alan *The Keys to Kabbalah* (4 volumes), 1996 Privately published discourse on the Ladder of Light: see http://www.soft.net.uk/ambain/webdoc2.htm

Knight, Gareth *Experience of the Inner Worlds: a course in Christian Qabalistic Magic,* Helios, 1975

Fiction

Banks, Iain M. *Feersum Endjinn,* Orbit, 1994

History

Cook, Roger *The Tree of Life: Image for the Cosmos,* Thames & Hudson, 1974

Freke, Timothy and Gandy, Peter *The Jesus Mysteries,* Thorsons, 1999

Hanson, Kenneth *Kabbalah: three thousand years of mystic tradition,* Council Oak, 1998

Howe, Ellic *The Magicians of the Golden Dawn,* RKP, 1972

Matthews, Caitlin & John *The Western Way Volume 2,* Arkana, 1986

McIntosh, Christopher *The Rosy Cross Unveiled,* Aquarian, 1980

Scholem, Gersholm *Origins of the Kabbalah* (Translated from the German by Allan Arkush), Princeton, 1990

Yates, Frances A. *Giordano Bruno and the Hermetic Tradition,* RKP, 1964

Human Potential

Ferrucci, Piero *What We May Be: the Visions and Techniques of Psychosynthesis,* Turnstone, 1982

Gawain, Shakti *Creative Visualization,* New World Library, 1978

Grasse, Ray *The Waking Dream,* Quest, 1996

Hoffman, Edward (ed.) *Opening the Inner Gates: New Paths in Kabbalah & Psychology,* Shambhala, 1995

Jeffers, Susan *End the Struggle and Dance with Life,* Hodder, 1996

Jung, Carl G. *Man and his Symbols,* Aldus, 1964

Keen, Sam *Hymns to an Unknown God: Awakening the Spirit in Everyday Life,* Piatkus, 1994

Parfitt, Will *Walking Through Walls,* 1990, Element

Tart, Charles *Waking Up: Overcoming the Obstacles to Human Potential,* Element, 1986

Kabbalah

Besserman, Perle *Kabbalah and Jewish Mysticism,* Shambhala, 1997

Epstein, Perle *Kabbalah: the Way of the Jewish Mystic,* Weiser, 1979

Fisdel, Steven A. *The Practice of Kabbalah,* Aranson, 1996

Halevi, Z'ev ben Shimon *The Way of Kabbalah,* Rider, 1976

Halevi, Z'ev ben Shimon *Kabbalah: Tradition of Hidden Knowledge,* Thames & Hudson, 1979

Halevi, Z'ev ben Shimon *Adam and the Kabbalistic Tree,* Gateway, 1985

Hoffman, Edward *The Way of Splendour: Jewish Mysticism and Modern Psychology,* Shambhala, 1981

Kaplan, Aryeh *Meditation and Kabbalah,* Weiser, 1985

Matt, Daniel C *The Essential Kabbalah: the Heart of Jewish Mysticism,* Castle, 1997

Ribner, Melinda *Everyday Kabbalah: a Practical Guide to Jewish Meditation, Healing and Personal Growth,* Citadel, 1998

Unterman, Alan *The Wisdom of the Jewish Mystics,* Sheldon, 1976

Occultism

Steiner, Rudolf *Occult Science: An Outline,* Steiner Press, 1972

Qabalah

Ashcroft-Nowicki, Dolores *The Shining Paths: an Experiential Journey through the Tree of Life,* Aquarian, 1983

Gray, William *The Ladder of Lights,* Weiser, 1968

Gray, William *The Tree of Evil,* Helios, 1974

Gray, William *The Talking Tree,* Weiser, 1977

King, Francis *Magic: the Western Tradition,* Thames & Hudson, 1975

Knight, Gareth *A Practical Guide to Qabalistic Symbolism* (2 volumes), Helios, 1976

Love, Jeff *The Quantum Gods: the Origin and Nature of Matter and Consciousness,* Compton Russell, 1976

Parfitt, Will *The New Living Qabalah,* Element, 1995

Ponce, Charles *Kabbalah – An Introduction and Illumination for the World Today,* Quest, 1997

Index